The New German
REICHSCHANCELLERY
In Berlin 1938 - 1945

by Ray & Josephine Cowdery

USM, Inc.
Rapid City SD USA
2003

United States Library of Congress Cataloging in Publication Data
USM, Inc.
International Standard Book Number (ISBN) 0-910667-28-4

    Cowdery, Ray R. 1941 -
    Cowdery, Josephine N. 1963 -

Title: *REICHSCHANCELLERY*
        First American Edition

1.   ARCHITECTURE, Germany, Europe, Berlin, Nazi
2.   HISTORY, Military, World War II, Nazi Party, Germany, Europe

Printed in Hong Kong
Copyright © 2003 by Ray & Josephine Cowdery All Rights Reserved

---

DISTRIBUTED EXCLUSIVELY WORLDWIDE BY:
USM Incorporated
Post Office Box 2600, Rapid City, SD 57709-2600 USA
www.usmbooks.com

PUBLISHER'S DECLARATION

The publisher and distributor of this book is USM, Inc., PO Box 2600, Rapid City, SD 57709-2600 USA, and they wish to make clear that this book was published in the United States of America for consumption by Americans who, through tradition and under the protection of the US Constitution and Bill of Rights are guaranteed certain absolute rights to freedom of speech and the press, and all the benefits that such rights imply.

It is the specific intent and desire of the publisher and distributor that this book NOT BE distributed and/or sold in Canada, Australia, Switzerland; countries of the European Union (EU), including but not limited to Austria, Belgium, Denmark, France, Germany, Italy, the Netherlands, Sweden, United Kingdom, etc., which do not have the same tradition mentioned above, and/or do not provide citizens with a similar right to freedom of speech, belief and expression, and where possession or distribution of literature which may depict any aspect of the German Third Reich in a neutral or positive way might be severely restricted by law, and could result in confiscation, a fine, incarceration, or all three.

Due to the controversial nature of the content of this book and the potential for misunderstanding portions appearing out of context, the copyright owners expressly forbid reproduction of any part of this book, the reproduction of which may tend to alter the original meaning of the larger portion from which the part was extracted. Excerpts published by others in reviews or in critical works which tend to alter the meaning of the general section from which they were taken, will be treated as violations of the rights of the copyright owners and pursued to the full extent of the law. No part of this book may be reproduced in any form without prior written permission from the copyright owners.

Publisher's declaration Copyright © 2003 USM, Inc.

PLEASE NOTE: the maps on the inside the front and back covers of this book show the Government Quarter of central Berlin in the late 1930s in great detail. The left side map provides the greatest detail while the one on the right shows much more of the city. To orient yourself, look first at the left hand map inside the front cover. Just below the large number 20 on the Spree River is the Reichstag and the Pariser Platz in front of the Brandenburger Gate. Just to the right of the large number 19 is the Reichschancellery and its garden.

The beautiful Lotar Müller illustration of the Voßstraße face of the New Reichschancellery on the title page of this book was originally used in the French tourist brochure of the city of Berlin published in 1939 by the Landesfremdenverkehrsverband Berlin at Klosterstraße 71, Berlin C2.

REICHSCHANCELLERY

The New German REICHSCHANCELLERY

PREFACE

In 1987 we wrote and published a 64 page, limited edition hardcover book about Adolf Hitler's New German Reichschancellery in Berlin for the relatively small group of people interested in such things at that time. Since then we have traveled back to Berlin dozens of times and acquired far greater knowledge of the subject and a much larger archive of associated material. In the same period interest in Hitler and the Reichschancellery has exploded as specialized TV networks and major book retailers have exploited the market for popular material regarding Hitler and Nazi Germany. This book has grown out of the many requests we have had to provide additional written and graphic material pertaining to the design and construction of the New Reichschancellery and the personalities involved with it.

We were on holidays in Berlin on 9 November 1989 as the Communist grip on much of the population of Europe finally loosened. That evening, as the Berlin Wall fell before hundreds of thousands in the cheering crowds, we realized that what remained of the site of the New Reichschancellery (accidentally preserved for many years by the sheer stupidity of the Communist regime in East Berlin) was doomed to certain destruction.

Unfortunately, we were right. In a very short time the cheap, small *"Socialist People's Paradise"* apartments that the East Berlin government had erected along the west side of Wilhelmstraße were surrounded by dozens of other construction sites for buildings that would eventually house much of the army of office workers in the new Berlin. They also obliterated much of the most interesting history in that enormously historic area.

Many of the dozens of trips we made to Berlin in the 1980s and 1990s we made as guides for hundreds of Americans on World War II history tours that we organized over a period of 16 years. The unquenchable interest our tour passengers had in the New Reichschancellery building and the people that inhabited it for the final 76 months of the Third Reich, convinced us of the need for an objective book that treated the subject in considerably more depth than our previous volume.

Listening to the opinions of those we guided to Berlin and to the site of the New Reichschancellery, we also came to the realization that most of them had great admiration for the building and wanted to stand on the spot where it once stood or carry away a tiny fragment of it. On the other hand, virtually all post-war English language art and architecture books which even bother to mention Third Reich architecture soundly condemn this work in the strongest terms. Deciding whether the New Reichschancellery is or is not great architecture is not the mission of this book. This book simply records a rare in-depth objective glimpse into that little-known palace that was for a few short years, the seat of the most powerful secular ruler in the history of Europe.

We wish to thank the following people who have assisted us with this book: Frank Knolle, Terry Eckert, Andreas Gronemann, Michael and Linda Kelly, Robert Wilson and Dan Youmell.

To orient yourself to the New Reichschancellery, we suggest you turn now to the page after 125.

Ray & Josephine Cowdery
Rapid City, South Dakota
2003

Some of the nine story apartment buildings erected on the site of the New Reichschancellery by the housing authority of East Berlin in 1987 and 1988 are shown at the left. The cars are parked along the north side of Voßstraße and Wilhelmstraße runs horizontally across the foreground. By walking past the white car and turning to the right, one can walk through an arched passage into the garden of these apartments to the very spot where the bodies of Eva and Adolf Hitler were exhumed by Soviet soldiers on 4 May 1945. A photograph of the apartment gardens may be found on page 110.

A few things you need to know to get the most from this book...

The German word *Führer* means "Leader" but during the Third Reich it was used almost exclusively in reference to Germany's 23rd Chancellor, Adolf Hitler. Under Germany's parliamentary system of government the Chancellor (*Kanzler* in German) was the chairman of the ministers that headed the various ministries that effectively ran the country. During his 12+ years as Chancellor of Germany, Hitler also held the office of State President and had total power to relieve or replace any or all of the government ministers.

The Chancellery (*Kanzlei* in German) of Germany was the building where affairs of government were conducted and the principal office and residence of the leader of the German government in Berlin. Starting in 1937 Hitler also had a second smaller Reichschancellery near the town of Berchtesgaden in Bayern, close to his private mountain home, the *Berghof* (see photo on page 116). The New Reichschancellery in Berlin was the first large smoke-free building in the western world.

The German letter ß is read and pronounced as a double-S and never as any other sound. These days two S letters are often substituted for the ß (the name of this letter is pronounced es-set) but during the Third Reich it was in common usage. For consistency we have elected to use a ß wherever one might have originally been found in German words during the period 1933 - 1945.

The German word *Reich* means "Empire" - the state or nation. For the sake of readability we have translated the word Reich as "State" in those cases where we have chosen to translate it at all.

All words and phrases found between square brackets [ ] in the text have been put there by the authors for the sake of clarity.

Collectors should be aware that there are literally tens of thousands of fake Reichschancellery souvenirs on the market around the world. There has been a certain fascination with the place from the day that Hitler moved in. From the moment American, British and other occupations troops and civilians began arriving in Berlin in the summer of 1945, underpaid Soviet soldiers were perfectly aware that their Allies would buy anything connected with Hitler and his Reichschancellery for cash.

The Russians took uncountable numbers of foreigners on tours of the Reichschancellery and the Hitler bunker (see page 107) before the site was leveled late in 1949. Each of the visitors had a chance to buy some of "Hitler's personal property". The Tiergarten public park adjacent to the Reichschancellery was the venue for a huge swapmeet and black market in the years following the collapse of the Third Reich and "Hitler relics" were readily available there. Among the most commonly counterfeited Reichschancellery items are silverware, coat check chips, meal tickets, dedication day souvenirs, etc.

The spectacular previously unpublished photograph above is actually two photographs - a two negative panorama looking east through the Brandenburger Gate and straight down Unter Den Linden. These historic photographs and others in this book identified as "Knolle photos" were taken in late summer and autumn of 1946 by US Army Air Force First Lieutenant (Byron F.) Frank Knolle. Knolle was stationed at Tempelhof Airfield in Berlin after the war and acquired an excellent Contax II camera with which he documented his stay. He met and married his army nurse wife there. We are greatly indebted to Frank Knolle for the use of his historic images, without which the story of the New Reichschancellery building would be incomplete.

The street running off to the right in front of the building at the right edge of the panorama was Hermann-Göring-Straße (today it is called Ebert-Straße).The crowd of people on the left behind the jeep is standing in the corner of the treeless Tiergarten, involved in what can best be described as a "swapmeet". In the fall of 1946 most Berliners were still destitute and if they had something to sell or barter, they came to the Tiergarten in central Berlin in the hope of finding a likely buyer.

The New German REICHSCHANCELLERY

BERLIN IN 1938

Berlin was at the crossroads of the Warsaw-Paris/Rome-Stockholm rail lines and the focal point of all European air traffic. Tempelhof airport was close to the center of the metropolis of 4-1/2 million people. Lakes, parks and rivers accessible in all parts of the city made Berlin the sports and recreation capital of the Reich as well as the cultural and governmental capital.

Colossal Olympic facilities designed by the March brothers and prepared for the XI Olympiad in 1936 survived World War II intact. They still testify to the methods and scale on which the Nazis built the structures they intended to use for a thousand years. Small and fragile are not words that come to mind.

Industry was welcome in the capital. The northwest Berlin suburb of Siemensstadt was not only the home of its namesake, but of giant Allgemeine Elektrische Gesellschaft (AEG), the Borsig Locomotive Works, Singer Sewing Machines and dozens of smaller industries as well. Schools, academies, zoos, museums, seminaries, libraries and galleries were spread throughout Berlin. At least eight government institutes and countless departments, ministries and bureaus were found there.

The Nazis had very grand ideas for the new Berlin they envisaged, and some of the plans had begun to take shape prior to the Russian/German invasion of Poland in September 1939. While Hitler busied himself with construction projects in München (Munich) and Nürnberg, Hermann Göring erected a new Air Ministry in Berlin based on designs of Ernst Sagebiel. The Deutschlandhalle followed. Many subsequent efforts in Berlin and throughout the Reich borrowed from the main features of Sagebiel's work; flat or hip-roofs and row after row of heavily accented, bordered windows. Although distinctly at odds with the classical building style of Schinkel, Unger, Knobelsdorff and Eosander, they will remain a prominent and obvious aspect of Berlin's architecture for a very long time to come.

Chancellor Adolf Hitler and his Reichschancellery architect, Albert Speer, in a photograph taken 12 November 1939.

HITLER'S ARCHITECT ALBERT SPEER

During the early 1930s while Hitler was building München and Nürnberg into cities of the Nazi Party he had admired and used the Münchener, Paul Ludwig Troost as his architect. Troost's untimely death on 21 January 1934 left a vacancy that was filled in large part by 29 year old architect, Albert Speer. Speer's willingness to carry on in the tradition of Troost and his unabashed admiration of Hitler made him the Führer's favorite.

Hitler's construction technique was not complex and is nicely summed up in his statement that, "natural stone and nordic hardburned bricks are our most durable building materials. The rule is that the most expensive material often proves to be the least expensive in the long run. The unconditional durability of construction material

Part of a postcard showing Berlin's famous Adlon Hotel at Pariser Platz 1 in front of the Brandenburger Gate, just a block away from the New Reichschancellery. About 1937.

The New German REICHSCHANCELLERY

A portion of architect Albert Speer's enormous model of the new Berlin shows the Government Quarter in great detail. The New Reichschancellery and its gardens can be seen in the center of the photo. Hermann-Göring-Straße runs right to left (north to south) in back of the Brandenburger Gate (right center) and intersects with Voßstraße at the far end of the New Reichschancellery. The street on the near side of the New Reichschancellery and its gardens is Wilhelmstraße and it intersects at the right edge of the photo with treelined Unter Den Linden. The model still exists in the City of Berlin Museum.

The octagonal square in the upper left is Leipziger Platz and beyond it lies the proposed Runder Platz. Under the New Reichschancellery garden were car bunkers belonging to the Leibstandarte SS Adolf Hitler Guard Detachment which was billeted in the two buildings on Hermann-Göring-Straße just to the right of the far end of the New Reichschancellery. The trees in the upper right quarter of this photograph represent a portion of the enormous Tiergarten public park. The map on the facing page identifies many of the buildings and streets you see on Speer's model, above. Try to orient yourself with the model and the map.

The New German RЄICHSCHANCЄLLЄRY

The Government Quarter

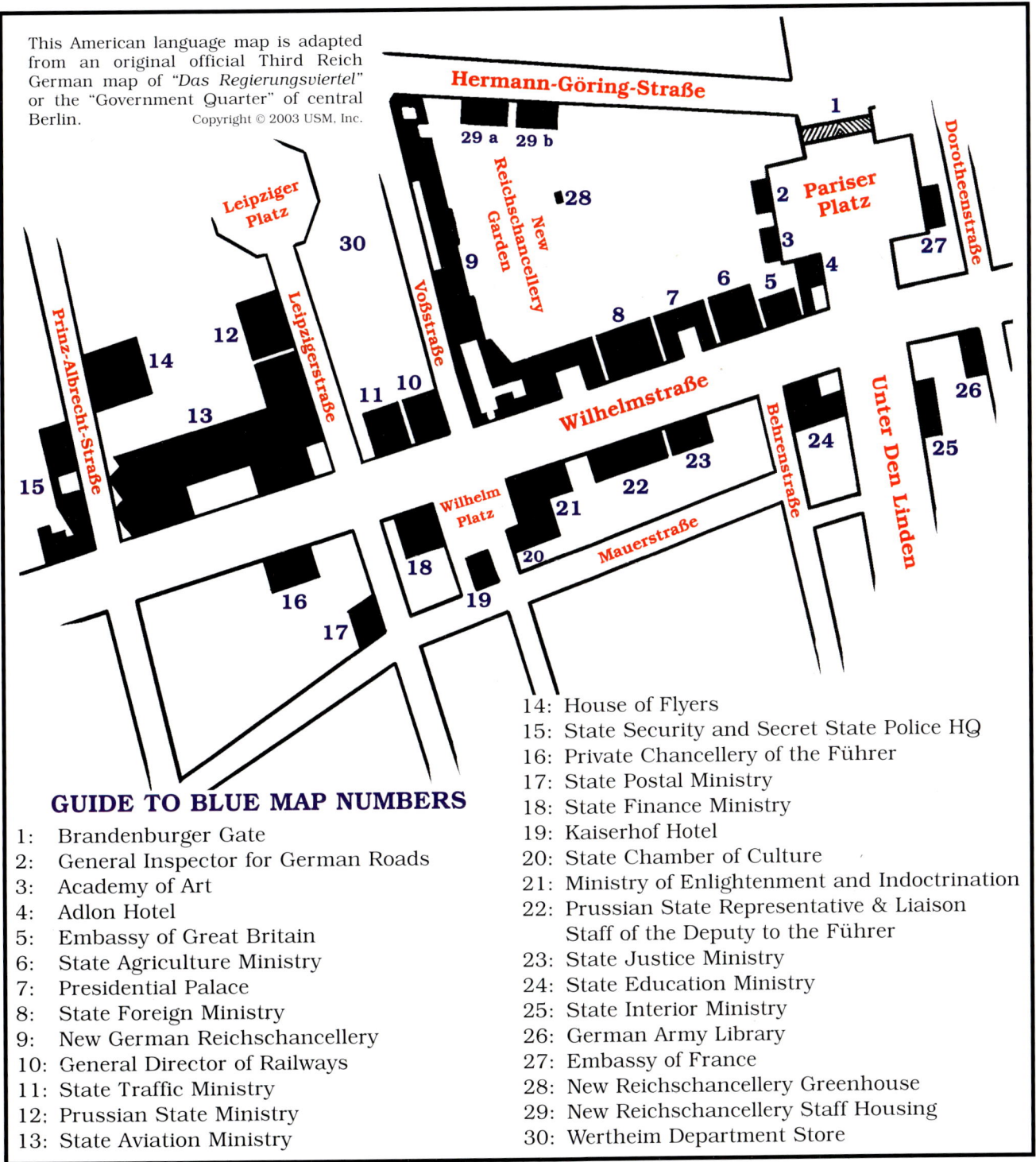

This American language map is adapted from an original official Third Reich German map of *"Das Regierungsviertel"* or the "Government Quarter" of central Berlin. Copyright © 2003 USM, Inc.

GUIDE TO BLUE MAP NUMBERS

1: Brandenburger Gate
2: General Inspector for German Roads
3: Academy of Art
4: Adlon Hotel
5: Embassy of Great Britain
6: State Agriculture Ministry
7: Presidential Palace
8: State Foreign Ministry
9: New German Reichschancellery
10: General Director of Railways
11: State Traffic Ministry
12: Prussian State Ministry
13: State Aviation Ministry
14: House of Flyers
15: State Security and Secret State Police HQ
16: Private Chancellery of the Führer
17: State Postal Ministry
18: State Finance Ministry
19: Kaiserhof Hotel
20: State Chamber of Culture
21: Ministry of Enlightenment and Indoctrination
22: Prussian State Representative & Liaison Staff of the Deputy to the Führer
23: State Justice Ministry
24: State Education Ministry
25: State Interior Ministry
26: German Army Library
27: Embassy of France
28: New Reichschancellery Greenhouse
29: New Reichschancellery Staff Housing
30: Wertheim Department Store

The New German RECHSCHANCELLERY

Speer looks on while Hitler illustrates a point with a sketch.

is the first technical consideration and always the supreme and decisive principle."

Prior to becoming the 23rd Chancellor of Germany, Hitler had written, "How truly pitiful the relationship between State and private builders has become. If the fate of Rome awaits Berlin, our descendants will have a few hotels and a couple of Jewish department stores to admire as examples of the grand construction and culture of our times."

Speer knew an opportunity when he saw one. After working with Hitler for a relatively short time he wrote, "What came more clearly into focus for me in the buildings which arose after the [Nazi] assumption of power were the austere and forceful designs that were never monotonous. They were simple and clear without the superfluous. Frugal in decoration but with each decoration having a place so that it could never be thought of as unneeded. Everything pure in material, form and outline.

"...the Führer occupied himself not only with the overall plans but with every detail. Each new material received his stamp of approval and many aspects were improved by his fruitful suggestions. Those hours of planning became hours of purest

PLAN OF THE OLD AND NEW REICHSCHANCELLERIES AND THEIR GARDENS

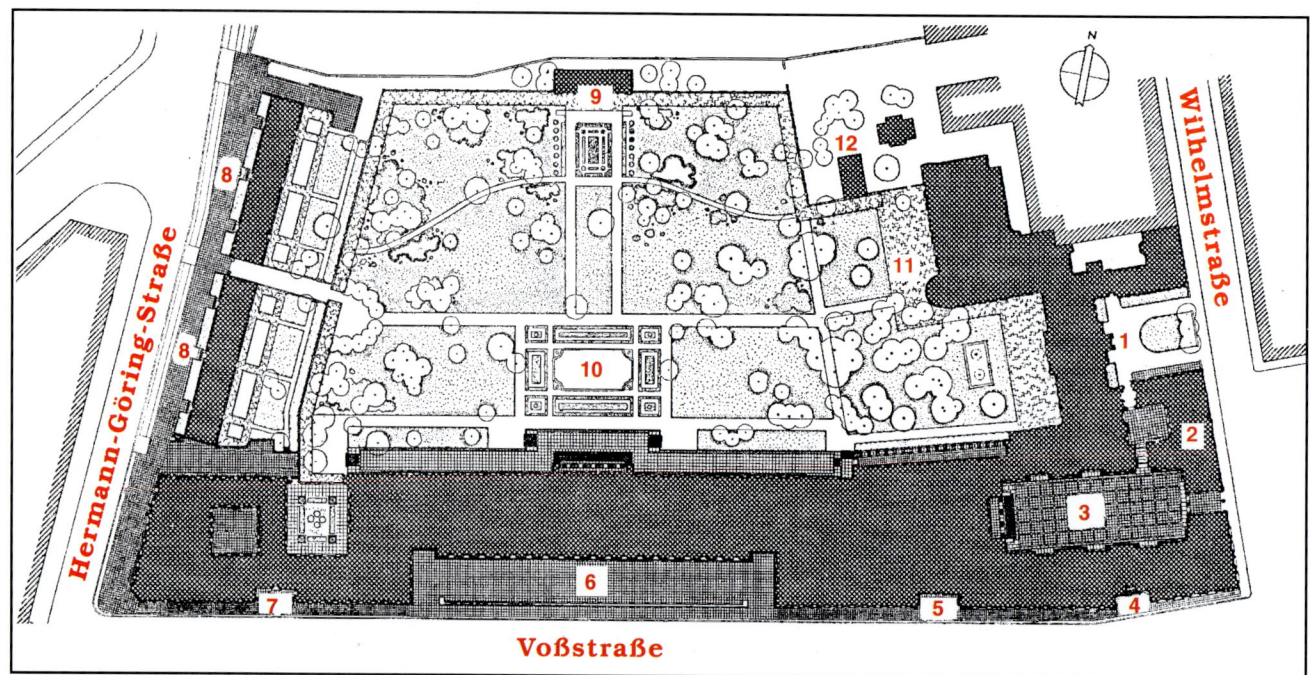

Red numbers indicate the following: 1) the Old Reichschancellery, 2) Old Reichschancellery addition 1929/30 with the Speer balcony on the front facing Wilhelmplatz across the street, 3) Honor Courtyard, 4) Entrance to the former Borsig Palace, 5) Voßstraße number 4 entrance to the New Reichschancellery, 6) Center-front, 7) Voßstraße number 6 entrance to the New Reichschancellery, 8) Leibstandarte SS Adolf Hitler Guard Detachment and Reichschancellery Staff housing, 9) New Reichschancellery Greenhouse, 10) Reflecting Pool, 11) Exit from the Hitler Bunker and trench where the burned Hitler corpses were found, 12) Officer's Quarters.

The New German REICHSCHANCELLERY

The 1929/30 addition to the Old Reichschancellery showing the balcony Albert Speer added in 1934. See also page 106. Just below and beyond it is the door that Speer widened to provide access into the Honor Courtyard from Wilhelmstraße.

joy and deep feelings of happiness for the Führer. They were relaxation of the purest kind from which he gathered new strength for other planning. In these few hours free of politics he had the chance to dedicate himself to the art of construction.

"Monumental edifices of National Socialism shall rise like the domes of the Middle Ages, towering over the gables of private houses, above healthy worker apartments and above the clean factories of our large cities.

"The tasks of the future are unimaginably large, but the Führer provided us with the courage required to deal with them when he made the following remark at the Nazi Party Day cultural meeting in 1935:"

'The people will grow to accommodate higher tasks, and there is no doubt that when the Almighty gives us the courage to demand the immortal, He will give our people the strength to fulfill the immortal.'

Speer was sure that he would be working as a builder in Berlin for quite some time, as Hitler had told him:

"You attracted my notice during our rounds. I was looking for an architect to whom I could entrust my building plans. I wanted someone young; for as you know these plans extend far into the future. I need someone who will be able to continue after my death with the authority I have conferred on him. I saw you as that man."

The New German REICHSCHANCELLERY

The impressive Voßstraße 6 entrance to the New Reichschancellery had a permanent SS guard.

THE NEW REICHSCHANCELLERY

Speer could never have guessed what was on Hitler's mind when the two met in January 1938. Hitler told Speer, "I have an urgent assignment for you. I shall be holding extremely important conferences in the near future. For these, I need grand halls and salons which will make an impression on people, especially on the smaller dignitaries. For the site I am placing the whole of Voßstraße at your disposal. The cost is immaterial, but the job must be completed very quickly and be of solid construction. How long do you need? For plans, blueprints, everything? Even a year and a half or two years would be too long for me. Can you be done by 10 January 1939? I want to hold the next diplomatic reception in the New Chancellery."

Speer began tearing down buildings along the north side of Voßstraße at once. At the same time he began to plan the new buildings. Because some components (like hand-knotted rugs) had very long delivery times, he had to specify their size and color before he designed the rooms into which they would fit. Work on underground bunkers began from sketches while Speer and his staff plunged ahead with exterior designs.

Speer decided the entry to the New Reichschancellery would be from Wilhelm Platz where visitors could drive through great gates into the Honor Courtyard. Large bronze doors straight ahead would open into a medium-sized reception room. Double doors over 17 feet high in the Reception Room would open into a large hall clad in mosaic. The visitor would then pass from the Mosaic Hall through a round room with a domed ceiling and see before him a huge gallery over 480 feet long (twice the length of the Hall of Mirrors at Versailles, France). The walk from the entrance to Hitler's Reception Room would be an incredible 725 feet. The rooms were to be done in a rich variety of materials and colors with deep window niches filtering the outside light.

Over 4500 workers labored in two shifts to complete the New Reichschancellery on time. Hitler followed the progress of the construction carefully and at one point commented, "This [construction project] is no longer [being carried out at] the American tempo; it [the pace of the construction] has become the German tempo. I like to think that I also accomplish more than other statesmen accomplish in the so-called democracies. I think

One of two watercolors by artist Paul Herrmann depicting early phases of the construction of the New Reichschancellery.

we are following a different tempo politically, and if it is possible to annex a country to the Reich in three or four days, it must be possible to erect a building in one or two years."

The finished building greatly surprised and impressed Hitler when Speer turned it over to him on 9 January 1939. He praised the "genius of the architect". He loved the long walk that state guests and diplomats would have to take before reaching his reception room. He thought the reception room too small and had plans drawn up to triple its size.

Hitler was very pleased with his office and especially with the inlay on his desk showing a sword half-drawn from its sheath. "Good, good", he said to Speer, "when diplomats sitting in front of me at this desk see that, they will learn to shiver and shake".

At a ceremony at the Deutschlandhalle near the Avus race course to thank those who had worked on the construction of the New Reichschancellery Hitler said:

"I stand here as the representative of the German people. And whenever I receive anyone in the Chancellery, it is not the private individual Adolf Hitler who receives him, but the Leader of the German nation - and therefore it is not I who receive him, but Germany through me. For that reason I want these rooms to be in keeping with their high mission. Every one of you has contributed and your contribution will speak to posterity of our times. This is the first architectural creation of the new Greater German Reich!

"This is the special and wonderful property of architecture: when the work has been done, a monument remains. That endures. It is something different from a pair of boots, which also can be made, but which the wearer wears out in a year or two and then throws away. This remains, and through the centuries will bear witness to all those who helped create it."

Readers will get a much better idea of the kind of place the New Reichschancellery was by examining our selection of photographs of it and the impressions of several people closely connected with the construction of the building. The following impressions of Reichschancellery visitors are translated from the German language.

The second of two watercolors by artist Paul Herrmann depicting early phases of the construction of the New Reichschancellery.

The New German REICHSCHANCELLERY

IMPRESSIONS OF ADOLF HITLER - FÜHRER AND CHANCELLOR OF GERMANY

At the time after he founded the new Reich [the "Second Reich"], when Bismarck decided to purchase Palais Radziwill for use as the *Reichskanzlerpalais*, his offices were located in the Foreign Office. The fact that the Radziwill was adjacent to the Foreign Ministry was probably the main reason for its acquisition, as the early 18th century building had very little practical office space.

A Heinrich Hoffmann portrait of Adolf Hitler, 23rd Chancellor of Germany.

The building had been the seat of a noble family for many years. While it had respectable outside facades the interior had been renovated and embellished many times. By the end of the 19th century it was so overloaded with stylishness that "gorgeous" plaster work hid all of the original materials and proportions. Even the Great Hall in which the Berliner Kongress had been held, did not escape this embellishment.

Unsightly wall brackets and oversized ventilation grills made from sheet metal must have been popular items at the time. The pictures on the walls were low quality pieces on loan from Prussian collections. Among the Chancellor portraits, only the big one of Bismarck by Lenbach had any artistic value at all.

The park in back of the building had been allowed to run wild. Somebody's aversion to replacing old trees with young, healthy ones had led to the practice of filling hollow trees with brick or concrete. Had this procedure been followed longer the place would have had the look of Houthulster Wood [a World War I battlefield in Belgium] after three years of British bombardment.

Prior to 1918, the Reichskanzlers occupying the place had kept it in reasonable repair but after the revolution of 1918 it began to deteriorate. In 1934 I decided to use the building in spite of its condition. The roof beams were rotted through and floor boards were turning to powder. There was a limit to the number of people that might occupy any room at the same time because of the danger of collapse. For example, the Kongresshall where all diplomatic receptions were held was certified by police for the occupancy of only 60 people.

A few months prior to reconstruction, over 100 guests and servers had been allowed to attend a reception for Reichspräsident von Hindenburg. When we later ripped out the floors we found that the beams consisted almost entirely of tinder that could be crushed easily by hand. Cloudbursts brought not only water from above but also water from below. From Wilhelmstraße, a creek flowed into the rooms below ground level. In bad cases water gushed freely from all structural openings including toilets.

Professor Paul Ludwig Troost refurbished this office in the Old Reichschancellery on Wilhelmstraße for Hitler in 1934.

My predecessors [previous Chancellors] could generally expect that their period of service would only last four to five months. As a result they saw no reason to clean away the grime of the previous occupant or try to leave the place in better shape than they found it. The world took so little notice of Germany in the 1920s and early 1930s that few representative duties needed to be carried out in Berlin anyway.

So, in 1934 we found the entire building in the advanced stages of decay: ceilings and floors rotted, wall coverings and carpets molded, and the whole place reeking with an intolerable, evil smell.

An excellent period photo of the front facade of the Kaiserhof Hotel which faced the Reichschancellery from across Wilhem Platz. This is the view that Hitler had as he waved to the the crowds from the Speer balcony.

The Reichschancellery had been built during a chaotic period and in 1934 it was a rundown block of offices on the Wilhelm Platz which on the outside looked like the warehouse of a soap company or the garage of a city fire brigade. On the inside it looked like a tuberculosis sanatorium. To make it useable again I gave it a general renovation at my own expense. The project was put in the hands of Professor Troost and had the following aims:

1) To the extent possible, move the living rooms and reception rooms to the lower ground floor.

2) To renovate the entire second floor for the use of the Reichschancellery.

Up until that time my working area had been a room facing Wilhelm Platz which could be equated to a tastelessly decorated office of the manager of a medium-size cigarette and tobacco-ware company. With the windows closed it was too hot to work in the room and if the windows were opened it was too noisy. By moving the facilities of the Reichschancellery into the ground floor space we gained office rooms on the garden side of the building through new construction. The Kongresshall, often never used all year, was destined to become the Cabinet Meeting Hall.

Still missing after reconstruction was a suitable room for large state diplomatic receptions so I decided that architect Professor Gall should build a room adequate for 200 people.

As a lack of convertible space was beginning to constrain the melding of offices of the Reichspresident and Reichschancellor and there was no room for the Army Adjutants Department, we acquired nearby Borsig Palace. Borsig Palace was unacceptable by today's standards but was tower-high over the miserable standards of our Reichschancellery built in the 1890s.

Thus Professor Speer was given his first order for the completion of work on the old Reichschancellery. In very short time and without changing either facade, Speer was able to connect the architecture of Lucac [Borsig Palace] with the "soap factory warehouse" on Wilhelmstraße. Large scale conversion of the interior space provided rooms for a presidential office, the Army, the SA and the Nazi Party. The old Reichschancellery building was given a balcony facing Wilhelm Platz, and the result was that it received

A remarkable photo taken the night of Adolf Hitler's 50th birthday parade down Wilhemstraße on 19 April 1939. From right to left you can see the balcony Albert Speer built on the face of the Old Reichschancellery, the double doors opening into the Honor Courtyard, and at the end of the building Voßstraße turning off to the right out of Wilhelm Platz.

The New German REICHSCHANCELLERY

its first good looking architectural element.

In spite of all this of course, extending the building could only be called a temporary solution. Two situations convinced me in January 1938 to provide a real solution:

1) To facilitate east-west traffic across Berlin, the Berlin City Building Direction stated its intention to lengthen Jägerstraße over the Ministers Gardens and the Tiergarten to effect a connection with Tiergartenstraße. It was my opinion that this plan was wrong so I ordered Speer to reduce traffic on Leipziger Straße and Unter Den Linden by creating a passage in a direct westerly direction from Wilhelm Platz. This meant that Voßstraße would no longer be a narrow pass-street but would take on the character of a big through-road.

   There could be no case made for destroying the Wertheim Department Store block [on the south side of Voßstraße] and requiring the government to pay them for rebuilding. The alternative was to tear down the Reichschancellery side of Voßstraße and rebuild it.

2) During December 1937 and January 1938 I decided to resolve the Austrian question and to bring the *Großdeutsches Reich* [Greater German State] into existence. There was no possible way that the old Reichschancellery could serve the office and representative needs of the new Reich.

Therefore, on 11 January 1938 I instructed my General Building Inspector, Professor Albert Speer to design and build a New Reichschancellery along the north side of Voßstraße, and to complete the project no later than 10 January 1939.

Leibstandarte SS Adolf Hitler Guards at their posts at the Voßstraße 6 (west) entrance of the New Reichschancellery.

An early postcard showing the beautiful Wertheim Department Store which faced Leipzigerstraße. The second front of the building was on the south side of Voßstraße facing the west entrance of the New Reichschancellery. Hitler widened Voßstraße to the north rather than the south, so the government would not have to tear down this beautiful old building and pay the Wertheim company to rebuild elsewhere.

Though Speer had dealt mentally with this and other large tasks before, the scope and duties of this work were gigantic while the time span to complete it was necessarily incredibly short. The destruction of the north side of Voßstraße could not be finished before the end of March at the earliest, leaving only nine months for construction. That this opus succeeded and how this project

The New German RЕICHSCHANCELLERY

The artwork above is the design for a mural which was painted on a wall of the Leibstandarte SS Adolf Hitler Guard Detachment transportation bunker behind the Hermann-Göring-Straße quarters of the staff, under the Reichschancellery garden. The bunker was closed and covered over at the end of World War II by Soviet forces and remained closed for the next 45 years. In June 1990 the bunker was accidentally rediscovered and opened briefly (photographs of the remains of this and other murals were taken at that time), only to be quickly reburied by embarrassed officials of the Berlin Archaeological Office.

was finished is a credit to the ingenious architect exclusively - to his artistic talents, his unheard-of organizational talents and to the diligence of his coworkers. The worker of Berlin has outdone himself on this building. I don't think there is any place on earth where such a huge labor project could even be considered. On the other hand, every social need of every worker on this building was attended to. The unique efficiency of the Berlin worker can only be imagined if you think of the difficulties of winter and the heavy attacks of frost.

The layout of the New Reichschancellery is based on the final purpose of clean large-scale spaces. The gigantic length of the building along Voßstraße is aesthetically outstanding and is intended to have a splendid effect. The groupings of rooms inside the New Reichschancellery from the Honor Courtyard to the end of the Marble Gallery correspond not only to their practical purpose but create a gorgeous effect. The decorations of the inner rooms by painters, sculptors, weavers and other artisans is outstanding, and in keeping with the very best traditions of German arts and crafts workers. The park inside the New Reichschancellery will not long remain a park as it too will soon become a building site. Time simply did not allow the simultaneous construction of the Festivity Hall which will be erected there, and it can not be finished sooner than another two years.

Looking ahead, we will build a totally new Reichschancellery sometime after 1950 which will provide a new artistic and professional benchmark for the genial architect and builder, Albert Speer.

IMPRESSIONS OF HERMANN GIESLER
ARCHITECT

Albert Speer has now completed the first national building of the Greater German Reich. With it he has brought continuity to the history of large-scale German construction. In a year of restlessness and nervousness while many of the nations around Germany mobilized militarily and were barely able to live in peace, we started and finished this grand building project. The wondrous discipline and powerful tension which was exemplified in the German people in 1938 are perpetuated in the New Reichschancellery, and this building symbolically reflects our other successes in the past year.

As a cultural achievement and a product of our tranquility and wealth, the building is a benchmark and a refutation of liberalistic concepts. It demonstrates the power of one people to "make history" with monumental thought, when inspired by epochal beliefs.

The New Reichschancellery was not an economically planned object approached from a materialistic point of view. The completion and utilization of this building were its destiny. This building entered into the history of the Greater German Reich only through the mighty political encounter [see bottom of page 21] within its walls, which served to perfect our Greater German Reich. The architect, his staff and all other participants in the construction of the New Reichschancellery have helped to make the mystery of power understandable to everyone. So it is, that the interest in this magnificent building is not limited only to Germany, but is obvious throughout the world.

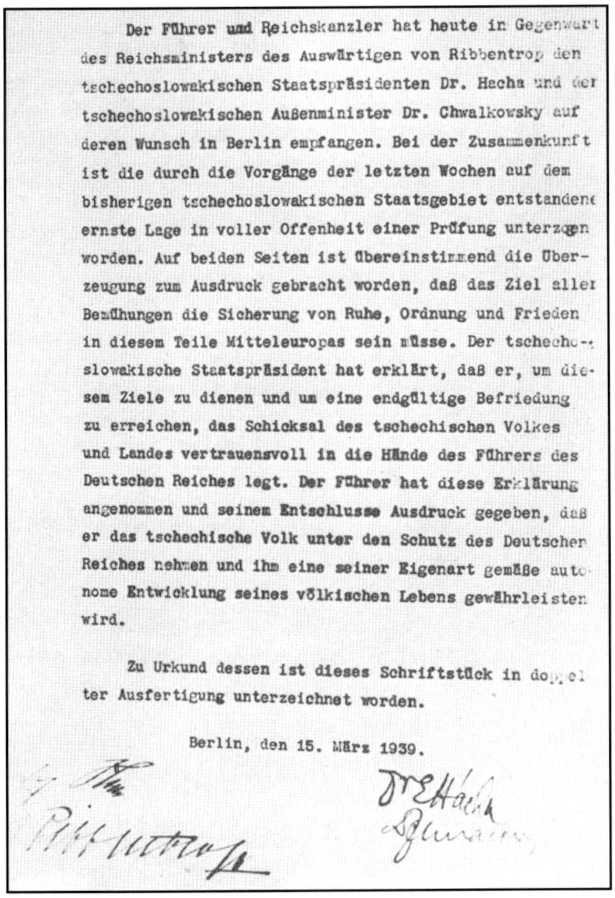

Der Führer und Reichskanzler hat heute in Gegenwart des Reichsministers des Auswärtigen von Ribbentrop den tschechoslowakischen Staatspräsidenten Dr. Hacha und den tschechoslowakischen Außenminister Dr. Chwalkowsky auf deren Wunsch in Berlin empfangen. Bei der Zusammenkunft ist die durch die Vorgänge der letzten Wochen auf dem bisherigen tschechoslowakischen Staatsgebiet entstandene ernste Lage in voller Offenheit einer Prüfung unterzogen worden. Auf beiden Seiten ist übereinstimmend die Überzeugung zum Ausdruck gebracht worden, daß das Ziel aller Bemühungen die Sicherung von Ruhe, Ordnung und Frieden in diesem Teile Mitteleuropas sein müsse. Der tschecho-slowakische Staatspräsident hat erklärt, daß er, um diesem Ziele zu dienen und um eine endgültige Befriedung zu erreichen, das Schicksal des tschechischen Volkes und Landes vertrauensvoll in die Hände des Führers des Deutschen Reiches legt. Der Führer hat diese Erklärung angenommen und seinem Entschlusse Ausdruck gegeben, daß er das tschechische Volk unter den Schutz des Deutschen Reiches nehmen und ihm eine seiner Eigenart gemäße autonome Entwicklung seines völkischen Lebens gewährleisten wird.

Zu Urkund dessen ist dieses Schriftstück in doppelter Ausfertigung unterzeichnet worden.

Berlin, den 15. März 1939.

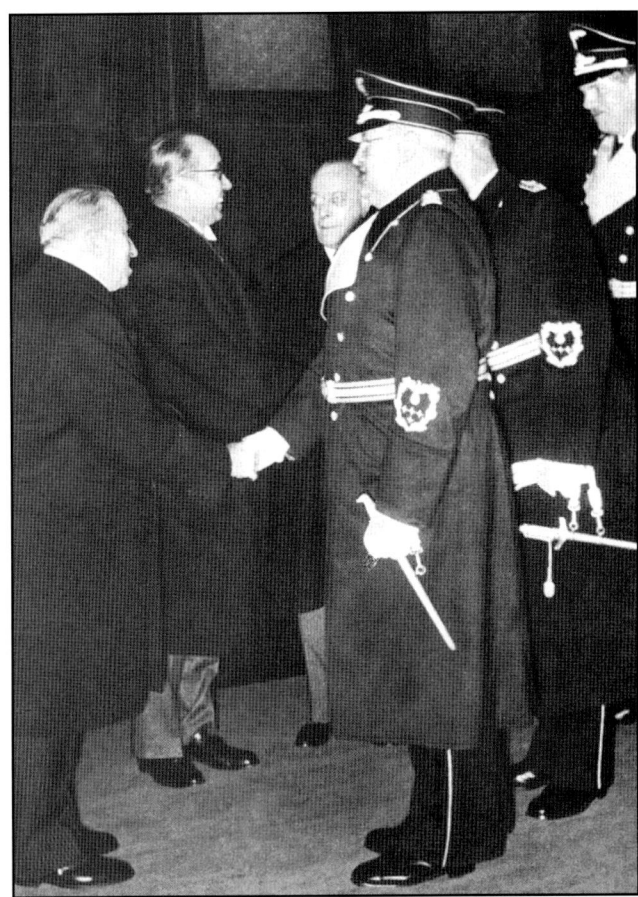

Dr. Emil Hácha, President of Czechoslovakia (at the left in the photo above) and his Foreign Minister Dr. Chvalkovsky being met in Berlin by very high ranking members of the German diplomatic corps. After a long session with Hitler in the New Reichschancellery, the parties signed the astonishing agreement (left above) which literally gave most of Czechoslovakia to Germany. Hácha felt there was no alternative in the wake of the British, French and Italian capitulation to Hitler a few months earlier in München. Hitler on the other hand, credited the intimidating effect of the New Reichschancellery as a principal reason that Dr. Hácha signed.

There are two places in Germany which serve the purposes of the Führer on behalf of the German people in a special way: the buildings of the Führer in München and the New Reichschancellery in Berlin. It is instructive today to contrast the buildings of architects Paul Ludwig Troost and Albert Speer, and to become conscious of the attitudes of the two masters as they demonstrate the political ascent of the Nazi Party and the country of Germany.

In München as in Berlin, the world-view and the power of the [Nazi] Party document themselves in our buildings. The buildings were born in times of great impulse and all are manifestations of National Socialism, which the outside world has opposed until now. The missing ingredient has now been materialized in stone by the Führer and provides proof of what he has been saying in his speeches.

The Nazi buildings in München are a symbol of our refound belief in a German future. Their ideological origins depict a fight for inner power, translated by Troost into uncompromising doric scarcity and strictness. The face of a fighting, combative Party.

Speer's New Reichschancellery on the other hand shows the grandeur and abundance of the Reich. Our enormously strong Reich expresses itself with a reserved presentation of worldly and universal greatness without giving up a single bit of true National Socialist character.

Being obliged to the people to give up the imperi-

NOTE: The "political encounter" Giesler aluded to on page 20 was the meeting of 15 March 1939 at the New Reichschancellery between Hitler and President Hácha of Czechoslovakia. In late 1938 Hitler demanded and got the Sudenten (German) parts of Czechoslovakia with the prior agreement of the leaders of Great Britain, France and Italy. On 15 March 1939 he demanded and got the provinces of Bohemia and Moravia. President Hácha was not easily convinced to give up the remainder of his country but Hitler felt that because Hácha had been intimidated by the New Reichschancellery, he capitulated. When Hácha signed Hitler's agreement, Slovakia became an independent country, Poland and Hungary grabbed sections they wanted and the rest of Czechoslovakia (Böhmen und Mähren or Bohemia and Moravia) became a Protectorate of Germany.

———— *The New German* RE̶I̶C̶H̶S̶C̶H̶A̶N̶C̶E̶L̶L̶E̶R̶Y̶ ————

The photograph above was taken from the middle of the open-air Honor Courtyard with its Arno Breker statues and entrance into the New Reichschancellery. The view was to the west. Below, are Speer's drawings of the Honor Courtyard entrance.

The New German REICHSCHANCELLERY

The Führerbau (Führer Building) on the Königsplatz in München was designed and built by Professor Paul Ludwig Troost as Hitler's office in the Capital of the Nazi Movement.

al representations found in the past in structurally materialistic buildings, the Führer further complicated the task of designing and erecting this magnificent building by requiring it be completed in just one year. Speer considered his problems and faced them squarely.

The task was to destroy a block of buildings from Wilhelm Platz along Voßstraße to the west and replace it with a complex, organically new building. He had to leave the lamentable building experiment of the Brüning period and also (out of civic pride) the Borsig Palace. Speer's consideration and innate sense preserved concrete examples of different worlds without detracting from the development of his own.

As Speer had already added the Führer balcony to the boring facade of the Old Reichschancellery in 1934, this facade was known well by every German and deemed worth preserving.

Beyond the balcony in the Honor Courtyard, Speer enriched the old facade with enormous double doors. Walking through these doors, one enters the New Reichschancellery and another world. The spirit of classically well balanced - masterly balanced - form overwhelms every visitor and he forgets the "flatness" he last observed outside. The strong form of the sculpted walls over which the ceiling flies like a sky, bespeaks a powerful dignity. Two figures by Arno Breker greatly increase the rhythm of the walls.

A close-up of "The Party", one of two Arno Breker statues flanking the huge door to the New Reichschancellery from the Honor Courtyard, shown on the facing page.

The master plan of the New Reichschancellery is best felt by experiencing the room-to-room sequence. A tension-rich change takes place at pleasant intervals; each room is completely individual in concept, yet all the rooms are linked by a close relationship and made fascinating by their paradoxes.

Part of the superiority of the design derives from its traditional start at the Wilhelm Platz: in surprising sequence rooms and halls parallel each other in two flights. They perfectly serve the concept of leading the visitor step-by-step to the Führer of the German people and the leader of the Greater German Reich, in a dignified manner. The visitor is compelled as he goes to change his gate from strolling or walking to pacing and finally to a strut.

The New German RElCHSCHANCELLERY

The head of an eagle like the one over the doorway in the Honor Courtyard of the New Reichschancellery by Professor Kurt Schmid-Ehmen.

This place is the technical rebirth of German majesty and grandeur. The scale used to build the old castles is exceeded; not in splendor or spatial extension, but by an obviously more comprehensive spiritual attitude. Here the idea rules. With great boldness, the idea grabs all the potential of materials and creation and makes them subservient.

The consideration with which the artistic elements are combined - the maturity of the works of sculptors and painters, the renaissance-like abundance and the richness of marble and mosaic, the craftsmanship of furniture makers, fabric weavers and carpet knotters; the precision of the metal workers and glass polishers - all this gives testimony to the Führer and the project, but also to artistic expression. It certainly gives testimony to organizational genius in the face of unique problems confronted for the first time, at the same time as regular problems that are dealt with by our General Construction Inspector [Speer].

I shall always remember the tension in the air on the day we came to Berlin with the Führer for the consecration of the new building - we all expected feverish activity; the final battle with time. We were amazed. What we found was quietness, everything in order, and that Speer had somehow finished the project a full day ahead of schedule. That one could finish this building in an organizational way is at least understandable, but to realize that young Speer and his co-workers had finished every last artistic detail, this is amazing. The National Socialist Speer, engages himself completely with enormous commitment and tenacity when he can serve the Führer, and accomplish that which seems to be impossible.

Speer's secret for mastering such a historical task? Germany has become *Großmacht* [a major world power] again. As a result of the feeling born in this knowledge and the security Speer found in it, the New Reichschancellery was created spontaneously, and when the Führer stands in it, he stands in front of the entire world! It is filled by an atmosphere of open broadmindedness without compromising a single aspect of German building principles. The facades tell us that by their

NEW REICHSCHANCELLERY FLOORPLAN

Maroon = Formal Presentation Rooms   Tan = Reichschancellery Staff and Administration Offices
Pink = Public Facilities   Blue = Floors, Hallways and Stairways   Gold = Work Rooms of the Führer and his Staff

1: Lobby of the Mosaic Hall
2: Mosaic Hall
3: Round Hall
4: Large Reception Hall
5: State Cabinet Hall
6: The Offices of Hitler and his Staff
7: Reichschancellery Dining Room
8: Courtyard of the Old Reichschancellery on Wilhelmstraße
9: Reflecting Pool in the Reichschancellery Garden
10: Housing of Reichschancellery Staff & SS Guard Detachment

The New German REICHSCHANCELLERY

A wide angle view of the entrance to the New Reichschancellery from the Honor Courtyard. This photograph was taken from very near the double doors on Wilhelmstraße through which automobiles could enter the Honor Courtyard. The view is west and the shadow indicates that the picture was taken just after noon. The Arno Breker statue on the left below, is called "The Party" and the one on the right is called "The Army". They may be seen in the photo above flanking the entrance to the New Reichschancellery.

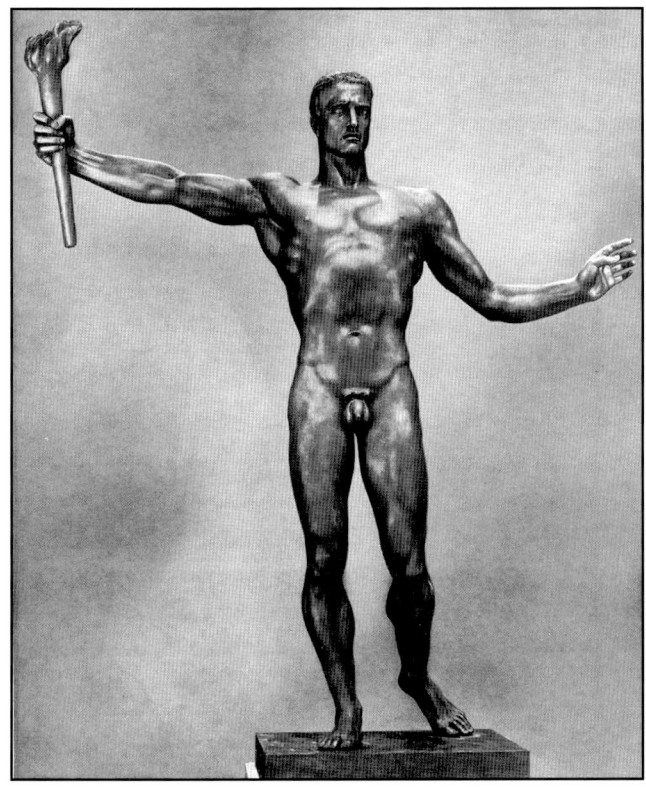

The New German REICHSCHANCELLERY

The picture above shows the "Vorhalle" or lobby of the Mosaic Hall in the New Reichschancellery. The door in the niche on the left opened into this lobby from the Honor Courtyard shown on pages 22 and 23. The door on the right opened directly into the enormous Mosaic Hall. The picture on the left below, shows the beautiful wall, floor, pillars and artificial skylight in the Mosaic Hall.

Prussian scarceness, which is often seen in the buildings of Gilly and Schinkel in Berlin. As the buildings of Brunellesco in Florence demonstrated his law against arbitrariness (and then created the possibility of alignment, and gave scales and buried validity again), so do the buildings of the Führer produce a picture of the future of architecture. The New Reichschancellery fulfills the demand of the Führer which he spoke of in his Cultural Speech of 1937. He said, "Our enemies will eventually understand this, but before they do all of our followers must know: the buildings of National Socialism emerge from the strengthening of our authority."

IMPRESSIONS OF RUDOLF WOLTERS

Even stronger than the powerful facade of the New Reichshancellery are the inner parts, which exude power and greatness and which could only have been born of our strong, self-confident era.

The complex urban facts which influenced the outer shape of the building - a long, stretched site narrowly limited between Wilhelm Platz, Voßstraße, the [Tiergarten] park and historical

The New German REICHSCHANCELLERY

The photograph above is a wide angle view of the Mosaic Hall taken from just inside its east doorway, showing the west end of the 150 foot long room. The architectural drawing at the right is Professor Albert Speer's design for the far end of the Mosaic Hall.

A close-up of Albert Speer's beautiful doorway at the west-end of the Mosaic Hall can be seen on page 28. The eagle by Kurt Schmid-Ehmen above the doorway was salvaged in 1945 by USAAF Colonel Edmund W. Hill and was on display for many years at the United States Air Force Museum in Dayton, Ohio. We are informed that it has now been put in "storage" and is no longer available for viewing by the public. See page 111.

Page 29 is a marvelous close-up of the mosaic and marble work in one of the panels of the south wall of the Mosaic Hall. To be absolutely specific, it is the mosaic panel at the near left end of the photograph at the top of this page.

The New German REICHSCHANCELLERY

The New German REICHSCHANCELLERY

The New German REICHSCHANCELLERY

Above, a close-up photograph of the floor in the Mosaic Hall which reflects the enormous artificial skylight ceiling 16 meters (52 feet) above. The squares in the floor were reddish-brown Saalburg Marble separated by mosaic bands.

Below, a photograph taken from the center of the Round Hall looking back into the Mosaic Hall. This connecting room was 14.25 meters (47 feet) in diameter and had walls covered in Austrian Marble. The Arno Breker relief sculpture above the door is called "The Genius" and is shown in far more detail at the top of the next column. At the bottom of the next column is the second Arno Breker relief sculpture in the Round Hall, this one called "The Fighter". See also page 91.

buildings - did not limit the spatial concepts of the designer. In fact, these constraints were made secondary by the sovereign will of Professor Speer, to a spacious interior that is without precedent in architecture.

The ground-plan [see plan on the bottom of page 24] clearly shows the spatial scaffolding of the whole: a representative axis running from Wilhelm Platz to Hermann-Göring-Straße along which everything falls into place in a self-evident way. The experience of a visitor who enters through the high bronze doors in the Honor Courtyard and journeys through five consecutive rooms, is similar to the experience of witnessing a festival drama. Each subsequent scene enlightens the others until all the elements are seen as a spirit filled, artistic whole.

Each room in the New Reichschancellery has its own personality and attitude, and each one plays on the others to improve the whole concept.

The New German REICHSCHANCELLERY

The New German REICHSCHANCELLERY

The Honor Courtyard with its stony pavement [see page 22 and 25] and the heavens arching above, prepares the concentration of the visitor. The ingeniously ordered walls of neutral gray stone give a balanced tranquility. Clear sculptures frame the heavy bronze doors of the portal, which is raised a few steps and outlined by massive stone pillars.

A marble clad lobby [see top of page 26] divides the Honor Courtyard from the Mosaic Hall. The mighty Mosaic Hall [see page 27] radiates "festival red" from its floors and walls. Huge mosaic surfaces by Kaspar are tastefully divided by almost invisible bands of marble. Marble plates with lighter mosaic dividers cover the floor. A richly structured ledge flies off the upper walls and supports an apparently weightless translucent ceiling. Heavy Roman-style door niches are set into the narrow sides of the room. Between identical sets of double red pillars at the far end of the Mosaic Hall is a bold, deep niche housing two tall mahogany doors. The door niche is framed by a heavy gray-green marble casing and over it stands a golden eagle, the work of Schmid-Ehmen.

From the softened light of this high hall one steps up into the Round Hall [see pages 30 and 31] which receives a bright even light through its dome. From its smooth multicolored marble walls to the freshness of the high relief sculptures above the doors, this fluid hall has a special unique character and charm that brings completeness to the room sequence. No one would notice that the architectural purpose of this room is as a link, to soften the awareness of the bend that Voßstraße

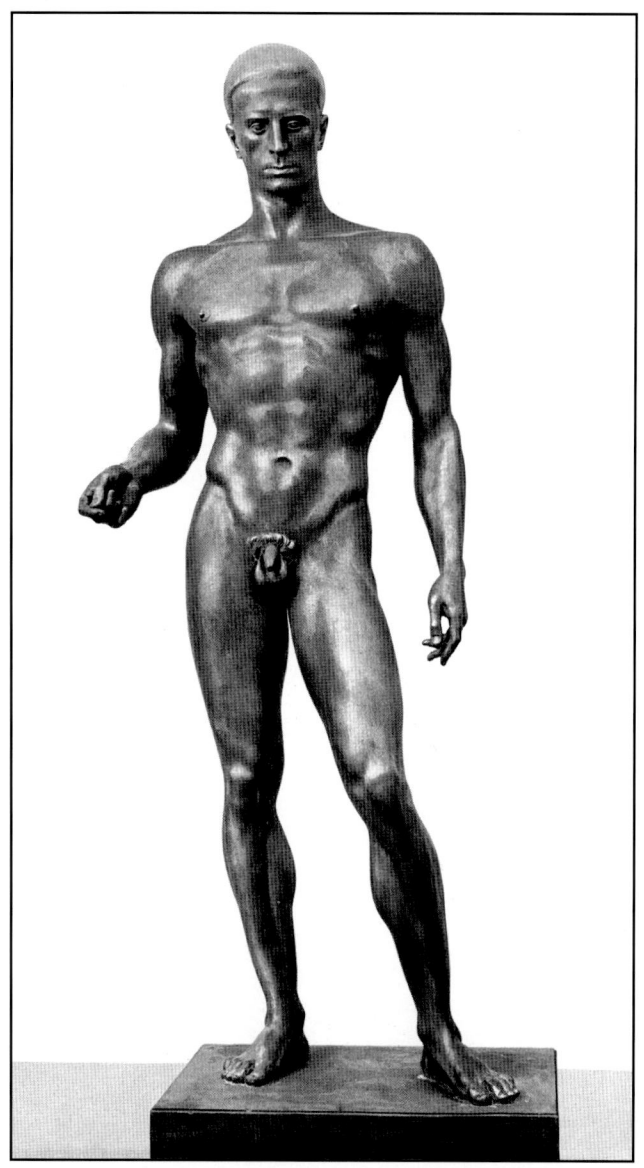

The Arno Breker statues above, "Thinker" and "Risk Taker", decorated the Round Hall.
The photo on page 33 was taken from just inside the east end of the Marble Gallery looking back into the Round Hall.

The New German REICHSCHANCELLERY

The New German REICHSCHANCELLERY

This photograph was taken from just inside the door shown on page 33 looking west down the full 479 foot length of the Marble Gallery. The Voßstraße windows are on the left and there are five doors on the right hand side. The center door (shown in greater detail on the facing page) opened into Hitler's Office. See page 107.

The New German REICHSCHANCELLERY

The New German REICHSCHANCELLERY

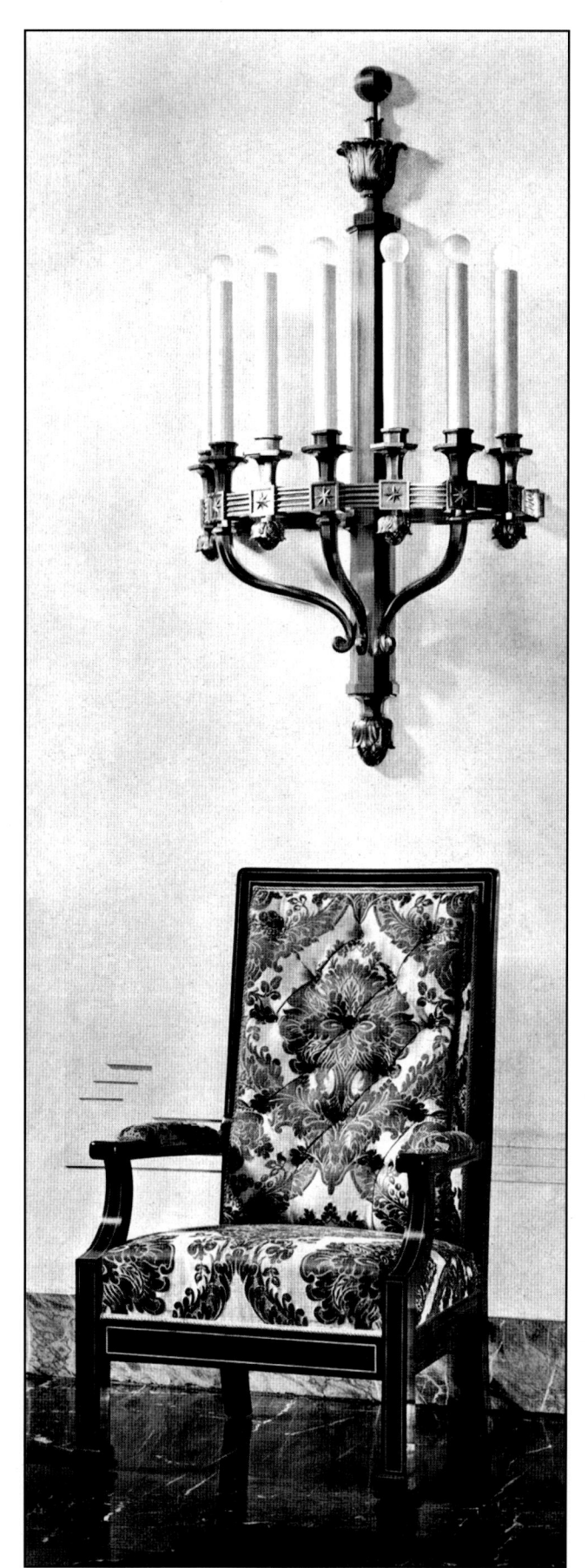

makes at this point.

A step through a doorway puts the visitor in the magnificent Marble Gallery [see page 34]. This tall, long room is also related to its position along Voßstraße, and is exclusively a transit room. The effect of the light filtering through 19 tall windows set deeply in marble niches on the left, is to create a wonderful alternating light and dark pattern. The large wall opposite holds huge tapestries by Professor Peiner. The center door [of five] in this wall enters directly into the Office of the Führer [see page 35] while the one at the far end leads to the Reception Room [see pages 40 and 41]. When the provisional furnishings in the Reception Room are removed and it is completed in the next year, it will become the focal point of the entire project.

This building was erected in only nine moths. In just a few weeks after completion, it served as the background for world-historic events and thus became historic itself. The rooms stand today in

The photograph at the left shows the detail in the upholstered chairs and wall sconces that lined the Marble Gallery.

The photo above shows a wooden cabinet supporting a bronze horse on a marble plinth in the Marble Gallery. The bronze grill of one of the Marble Gallery radiators is shown below.

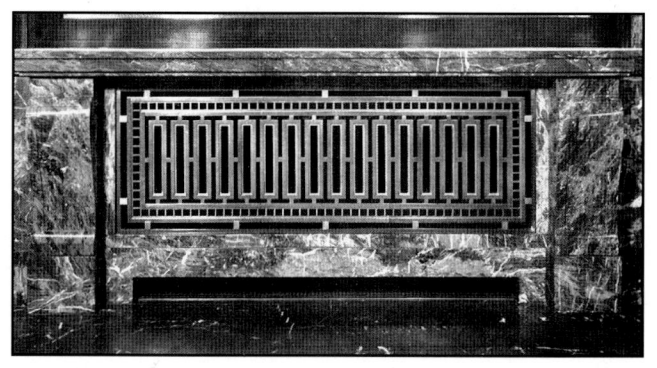

The New German REICHSCHANCELLERY

self-evident beauty and greatness. The minute details of the exterior forms; the entire interior with the works of painters, sculptors and craftsmen melts into one wonderful opus. For us, the architect's organizational performance is less an astonishing phenomenon than Speer's instinctive certainty, his artistic fanaticism and the trustworthiness of his feeling for form.

The accomplishment of Albert Speer in the construction of the New Reichschancellery cannot be explained as a response to the greatness and need of our time alone. It is also a willing and unselfish performance in fulfillment of an order by the Construction Master of the Reich. As an architect, Speer originates from the Nazi Party. His great works were the spectacular rallies of the Party. The [air] field at Tempelhof and Bücheberg stand out. Huge flags, masts, platforms and search lights [right] were the elements with which

The Speer "Dome of Light" shown at the right lit up the Reichsparteitag der Ehre (Reichs Party Day of Honor) in Nürnberg, from 8 to 14 September 1936. Below, a spectacular couch in the Marble Gallery under one of the enormous tapestries to be replaced with a new one by Professor Peiner. See page 123.

The New German REICHSCHANCELLERY

The New German REICHSCHANCELLERY

A typical furniture grouping outside an office door in the Marble Gallery. Visitors to offices or staff in the New Reichschancellery could await their appointment in comfort as long as they didn't smoke! Public areas of the Reichschancellery were smoke-free.

the architect formed his first big rooms. Photos of these examples have a "stony" form as did the arena for our Reichs Party Day meetings.

The New Reichschancellery is Speer's first opportunity to work in real stone and shows its relationship to his prior work in softer elements. Here in the inner part of the building one can actually feel the marching steps of the [Nazi] Movement. The architect found a new form which symbolizes the Greater German Reich. In this symbolism lies the secret of power that touches everyone who enters this house.

The New Reichschancellery is the premier state building and stands at the forefront of a building epoch that can and will stand any comparison with the biggest building epochs of world history. The form and sequence in which future construction activity will develop are predetermined by it.

Page 38 is a rarely seen photograph showing close-up details of the doors, marble door casing, wall sconces, wall treatment, ceiling treatment and furnishings in the Marble Gallery. Many of the items in this photograph can be seen in the photo above and photographs on page 36 and page 37. The gold cartouche above the doorway is the work of sculptor Hans Vogel.

IMPRESSIONS OF HERMANN KASPAR
ARCHITECTURAL PAINTER & MURALIST

Those who are willing to theorize with regard to the field of art are popularly known as "art advocates". This derogatory but striking expression reminds one of the well known advice Goethe gave on the subject of artistic eloquence:

"Educated artists do not lecture - they paint."

So we see, that there is almost no valid reason why a pictorial artist should speak at length and try to instruct others on art in general. It could only happen in extraordinary circumstances that a pictorial artist would become a lecturer and ask his audience to listen instead of contemplating his work. These are extraordinary circumstances.

There is a question worth asking; a timely question the urgency of which can not be doubted, and one which is clearly and unequivocally a question of our time:

"Does the modernization of our time and people find living expression in contemporary German

The Large Reception Room opened off the extreme west end of the Marble Gallery. Entry from the Marble Gallery was through the door near the corner. The door at the left edge of the photograph above opened into the Reichs Cabinet Hall.

art? Will future generations come to feel something of what we were when they contemplate the art we leave to them?"

The answer to this question can best be given by undertaking an exhaustive study of that branch of art which serves as a connecting link between the artistic expression of framed paintings and architecture - architectural painting and decorating.

Architecture is the mother of art. From her must come the seed for painting. Art will become visible first in architecture as a baby first becomes visible inside the form of the mother. Wall paintings, mosaics, frescoes, tapestries, and the like are the children of architecture. Architecture transfers its elements of size, spacial relationships and color to the artistic decorations that will eventually compliment it, just as the children of a mother display her characteristics.

Although this law of the birth of art is an eternal one it must be rethought in each new generation.

The language of our architectural painting cannot be like an informal conversation between good friends, but must be solemn and recognize the enormous responsibility it takes as it helps to form the will of expression of the people. The awesome duty to retain the right path will often fall in the hands of a single artist.

The form of a body being painted on a wall cannot be a simple duplicate of a model, but must be the synthesis of an infinite number of bodies contained in the mind and imagination of an artist. In the manner of a poet, a head must be the sum of a hundred heads, a leg the extract of a hundred legs. The image of humans painted on walls can neither be photographic nor artificially posed. Rather, it must be the artistic image demanded by its mother - the architecture into which it will fit. Also, things like draperies cannot simply be painted on but must support the rhythmic motion of the other elements with which they will function. Colors of paintings may not be selected arbitrarily, but must find their source in the colors of the room as it is the mission of the accent colors to intensify the basic room colors.

In the same way that the authoritarian state must be independent from considerations about insignificant individual interests and serve a higher ideal, so also must architectural painting be free to fill its natural place in the order of things. This sort of independence speaks from every old and monumental work of art even if that art is an idealization of a very narrow point of view.

By this process, contemporary works that succeed in achieving truly monumental status will always be seen as representing an accurate impression of the period in which they were done. The monumental does not always have to be large - even small scale monumental art identifies itself by its imaginative element and the superior mastery of all the forms it contains. As nature blooms in spring, so also must a monumental painting grow naturally and proclaim itself through firm form and color.

Architectural painting done in this way will always provide impulses to the artists of framed paintings. In earlier times the differences between monumental paintings and framed paintings was not as essential as it is now. When the structure of painting changed in the modern era, the two types became more separate. The great limitation to the use of the rich designs in monumental wall paintings is that their dimensions are limited by the architecture that they must fit within. The limitations of the form are the square, the rectangle and the circle and they lend themselves to the depiction of themes that portray the simplest forms of life:

1. The heroic posture
2. Peaceful views, and
3. Work

The theme of work will never be allotted the large spaces required for pictorial art as there is little historic basis for it. Although working and fighting have been the starting point of all life since the

A cozy seating area just inside the door of the Large Reception Hall in the New Reichschancellery.

The New German REICHSCHANCELLERY

The Reichs Cabinet Hall in the New Reichschancellery. Not shown in this photo are windows on the right which opened into a courtyard off the Reichschancellery garden. The photograph at the top of page 43 provides close-up details of the woven chair backs and portfolios of Cabinet members.

The New German REICHSCHANCELLERY

beginning of time, art was thought to serve the divine and the heroic, and to bring joy. Therefore, it is difficult to propose to fill the recreation rooms of workers with themes that depict the activities they are resting from.

A big role in room decoration themes should be given to depicting the [Party] symbol [the eagle and swastika] which in its mission transforms real emotion and information into a mental concept. Another concept certain to emerge stronger in the future than in the past will be the development of "cells of culture" which will be provisional offices on building sites where the staffs of painters and sculptors can work in complete harmony with the architect to design and implement large scale ornamentation. It is only natural that this cell structure would improve the results and reduce the problems of the artists working on a huge project together. In some ways this will be a vastly expanded version of the "huts" built around great construction projects of medieval times.

IMPRESSIONS OF DR. WILHELM LOTZ

The New Reichschancellery occupies the entire north side of Voßstraße between Wilhelmstraße on the east, and Hermann-Göring-Straße on the west. It provides a fitting and dignified finish for the historic quarter containing the German ministerial offices and their lovely gardens. Thus, the boundaries enclose a large trapezoid-shaped area with the longest side being Voßstraße at 421 meters [1381 feet, almost a quarter of a mile]. The

A close-up of the globe in the Reichs Cabinet Hall. A wide angle view of the same portion of this room may be seen on the next page. There was a similar globe in Hitler's office.

The New German REICHSCHANCELLERY

The Reichschancellery Cabinet Hall. The Reichschancellery Garden was outside the far wall. The wall on the left was made up of four windows that opened to a small courtyard. The globe shown on page 43 can be seen near the left edge of this photo.

eastern side is the site of the old Reichschancellery while along Hermann-Göring-Straße one finds the apartments of the Führer's guard detachment.

The strongest feature of this new building must be the facade along the Voßstraße front [see page 14]. This strong mass is divided into three sections of about equal length and roughly 22 meters [72 feet] high. The center portion is set back 16 meters [52 feet] from the ends and thereby widens Voßstraße at that point. Behind this facade are the working offices of the Führer and of his Adjutants, the Reichs Cabinet Hall, the Reception Room and the great Marble Gallery which runs as a huge corridor in front of the rooms. At each end on the street side are the various working offices of the staff of the Reichschancellery.

A visitor to this building would enter through the new double entry at Wilhelm Platz [see page 81] and find himself walking straight along the axis of the great halls which have a total length of over 300 meters [984 feet]. First, one enters the Honor Courtyard [see page 22-25] which measures 68 meters [223 feet] long by 26 meters [85 feet] wide.

The walls of the courtyard are of *Jura Dolomite* and consist of broad surfaces broken by columns 12.75 meters [42 feet] high. The columns carry a ledge rising to over 18 meters [59 feet].

To the sides of the Reichschancellery doorway stand sculptures by Professor Breker representing the Army and the Party [see page 25]. The Führer has said that they are among the most beautiful sculptures ever created in Germany. The doorway itself is framed by four large columns. Behind the columns on the face of the building above the doors is the national emblem [eagle and swastika] sculpted by Professor Schmid-Ehmen. The floor of the entrance is covered by mosaic ornaments made from the designs of Professor Kaspar. Stepping through the entrance the guest finds himself in a lobby [see page 26] with light red walls of *Unterberger Marble* and a darker red floor of *Saalburg Marble*.

The distinctive appearance of the next room is the result of the employment of a noble technique which was nearly lost in the last decades, but has once again found honor - the mosaic. The Mosaic Hall [see page 27] with a length of 46.2 meters

The New German REICHSCHANCELLERY

The northwest corner of Adolf Hitler's office in the New Reichschancellery was where he placed his desk. Looking to his left out the window gave him a view of the Reichschancellery garden and the greenhouse across it, in the distance.

The New German REICHSCHANCELLERY

The New German REICHSCHANCELLERY

The color photo on page 46 shows the view from Hitler's office desk looking to the east. On the left was Hitler's map desk and five windows overlooking the Reichschancellery Garden. Straight ahead was the Lenbach portrait of Bismarck hanging above the fireplace. On the right was the door (shown in detail above) that opened into the Marble Gallery.

The New German REICHSCHANCELLERY

The New German REICHSCHANCELLERY

The New German REICHSCHANCELLERY

The photograph on page 48 shows the conversation area in front of the fireplace at the east end of Hitler's office. The photograph on page 49 is a close-up of the fireplace and the Lenbach portrait of Bismarck that Hitler liked so much. The two panels above are Richard Klein's cast iron side plates by Lauchhammer inside the fireplace, which can not be seen in the photo on page 49.

The picture on page 51 shows the long map table on the window side of Hitler's office. Careful examination reveals a white SS Allach statue of Frederick the Great upon his horse in the middle of the table. An ad for the same Allach statute appears below.

[151 feet] and a width of 19.2 meters [63 feet] allows the mosaic technique a wondrous range of application. Bands of very special Austrian *Rotgrau Schnöll Marble* segment the room at a height of 13.5 meters [44 feet] and the fields within the bands (varying in width from 2.70 meters [9 feet] to 8.45 meters [28 feet]) carry mosaics designed by Professor Kaspar. Light gray and gold heraldic eagles in ornamental frames leap from the red background.

The floor of the Mosaic Hall is old-red [reddish-brown] *Saalburg Marble* with marble mosaics. The sovereign emblems [eagles with swastikas] above the doors are the work of Professor Schmid-Ehmen. The artificial skylight in this room is 16

The New German REICHSCHANCELLERY

The New German REICHSCHANCELLERY

The photograph above shows the cabinet and tapestry just behind Hitler's desk, which can be seen in the picture on page 45. Detail of the door behind his office desk is shown on page 53.

The New German REICHSCHANCELLERY

A close-up photograph of Hitler's New Reichschancellery desk and the inlay work which he felt would make some visitors "shiver and shake". The desk was manufactured in München by the Vereinigte Werkstätten. The desk still exists and was examined by the authors in München in January 1994. Close-ups of the inlay work are shown on page 55.

meters [52 feet] above the floor and utilizes indirect lights at the edges and spotlights from above to create a natural appearance.

The Round Hall [see page 30] is next and its skylight dome is also 16 meters [52 feet] high. This room is 14.25 meters [47 feet] in diameter and the columns and walls are all made of Austrian marble. Both the *Rotkopf* red marble and the *Kirchbruch* light gray marble occur naturally in the same area in Austria. The floor is *Saalburg Marble* with marble mosaics. The designs for the floor mosaics and the ceiling paintings were done by Professor Kaspar. Professor Breker created the fields over the doors and the light marble relief sculptures that fill them. The skylight is lit in a manner similar to the one in the Mosaic Hall.

Our next steps take us into the Marble Gallery [see page 34] and the center part of the New Reichschancellery. The high windows open directly to Voßstraße. The opposite side of this 146 meter [479 feet] by 12 meter [40 feet] room has immediate access to the Office of the Führer. Jutting out from the light marble walls are the heavy window and door frames in Deutsch-rot [dark red] marble. The windows of dark wood are set back over 2 meters [nearly 7 feet] and each one measures 2.35 meters [8 feet] by 6 meters [19 feet].

Eventually large tapestries made from new designs [see page 121] will decorate the huge marble walls, but for the present they display tapestries depicting scenes from the life of Alexander the Great, obtained from the Art History Museum in Wien [Vienna]. Over both access doors are sovereign eagles by Professor Schmid-Ehmen and over the other doors are cartouches by sculptor Hans Vogel.

The center door in the Marble Gallery [see page 35] opens into the Office of the Führer [see page 45] and one immediately sees the 2 meter high by 6 meter wide [6-1/2 x 9 feet] double glass doors on the garden side. The central position of the Office of the Führer in the organism of the new building is thus stressed on both the inside and the outside. The room is 27 meters in length by 14-1/2 meters wide [88-1/2 x 47-1/2 feet], and

The New German REICHSCHANCELLERY

the ceiling height is 9-3/4 meters [32 feet]. The walls consist of *Linbach Marble* [dark red] from Austria containing wooden insets. The floor is *Ruhpolding Marble* in geometric patterns.

In a corner stands the desk of the Führer. Across the way is a 3-1/4 meter wide by 2.7 meter high [10-1/2 x 8-3/4 feet] marble fireplace built into the wall. The fireplace plates were cast in iron from relief patterns by Professor Klein. The ceiling in the Führer's Office is made in cassettes of palisander wood inlayed with other woods. A wooden Schmid-Ehmen eagle covered in gold-leaf is positioned over the main entrance while cartouches by Professor Klein hang above the other doors.

To the west of the Führer's Office is the Cabinet Meeting Hall and in front of it, the Reichs Cabinet Hall. Immediately to the east of the Office of the

The New German REICHSCHANCELLERY

The east end of the New Reichschancellery Library showing the beautiful inlay work on the archival drawers beneath the glass doors on the book cabinets. This picture was taken before the decorative painting of the ceiling was begun.

The New German REICHSCHANCELLERY

Führer is the 48 meter by 10.20 meter [157 x 33 feet] Dining Room facing the garden. The ceiling has a height of 5 meters [16 feet] and the walls are wood paneled and finished with light green colored varnish. Via a wide stairway one reaches the library. This room is 55.5 meters long by 7.4 meters [182 x 24 feet] wide and is lined with cedar shelves to a height of 5 meters [16 feet]. In several niches are large china vases from the State China Factory in Nymphenburg, and soon the vaulted ceiling will have frescoes by Professor Hermann Kaspar. A last nearby room of substantial interest is the Model Hall where models of our great buildings of the future are kept.

Translation Copyright © 2003 by Ray & Josephine Cowdery

Nymphenburg Porzellan

Above, the same Nymphenburg porcelain vase shown in the photograph on page 56, is shown here in greater detail in its niche in the New Reichschancellery Library book cabinets. Nymphenburg porcelain was made at the very old National Porcelain Factory in the Nymphenburg section of München.

Left, a photograph of the hallway between the New Reichschancellery and Adolf Hitler's private suite of rooms in the former Radziwill Palais at Wilhelmstraße 77. Be sure to notice the three Spinn Workshop chandeliers hanging from the ceiling of this transitional hallway. The photograph for the Spinn Workshop advertisement shown on page 88 was taken in this hallway.

The New German RЄICHSCHANCЄLLЄRY

The desk and conversation area in the beautiful walnut office of State Minister Dr. Otto Meissner. Page 59 is a view looking east just inside the Voßstraße 4 entrance to the New Reichschancellery. A visitor entering from Voßstraße on the right and passing through the columns on the left would enter a hallway that would take him into the lobby of the Mosaic Hall shown on page 26.

The New German REICHSCHANCELLERY

The New German REICHSCHANCELLERY

A splendid view of the long hallway just inside the New Reichschancellery at the Voßstraße 6 entrance. Page 61 shows a rare glimpse of the stairway between the Dining Room and the Library in the New Reichschancellery.

The New German REICHSCHANCELLERY

The New German REICHSCHANCELLERY

The Dining Room in the New Reichschancellery faced the garden in the section connecting the old Borsig Palace to the New Reichschancellery. The dimensions of the Dining Room were 48 x 10.2 meters (157 x 33 feet) and it had a 5 meter (16 foot) ceiling.

The New German REICHSCHANCELLERY

The photograph above provides readers with a close-up view of a set table in the New Reichschancellery Dining Room. The room that can be seen through the open door at the top of the steps is the Lobby of the Mosaic Hall. Compare the table and doors in the distance with those in the photograph at the top of page 26.

NEW REICHSCHANCELLERY EXTERIORS

A close-up of the splendid Kurt Schmid-Ehmen eagle above the Voßstraße 6 entrance to the New Reichschancellery. Below, one of two Josef Thorak bronze horses on the terrace just outside the windows of Adolf Hitler's Office.

The New German REICHSCHANCELLERY

An excellent view of the terrace in the New Reichschancellery garden outside the north window wall of Hitler's Office. Hitler's Office had five huge windows/doors that opened out between and behind the pairs of columns above the terrace. Marmor und Natursteinwerke Josef Zander manufactured the columns and produced an advertisement to publicize the fact. You can find a reproduction of the advertisement on page 90.

In this view, you can also see both of the bronze horses by sculptor Josef Thorak, and beyond them the west end of the arched walkway (see page 66) that ran the entire length of the window wall of the New Reichschancellery Dining Room. To the left of the lamp post along the path, is the corner of the reflecting pool.

The New German Reichschancellery

*The arched walkway outside the window wall of the New Reichschancellery Dining Room.
Below, a view of Hitler's Office as seen from near the Greenhouse across the Reichschancellery garden.*

The New German REICHSCHANCELLERY

The off side of the same Thorak horse shown on the bottom of page 64. The buildings in the distance beyond the reflecting pool are the quarters of the Leibstandarte SS Adolf Hitler Guard Detachment and the New Reichschancellery Staff.

The New German REICHSCHANCELLERY

The spectacular arched walkway that ran the full 157 foot length of the garden side of the New Reichschancellery Dining Room. It must have been a remarkable sight when lit at night. The photographs on page 69 show two views of the greenhouse across the garden from the arched walkway.

The New German REICHSCHANCELLERY

The New German REICHSCHANCELLERY

An interior photograph of the enormous "Wintergarten" or greenhouse in the New Reichschancellery garden. The windows on the right in this photograph faced south, directly toward the windows on the north side of Hitler's Office on the back side of the New Reichschancellery building. The greenhouse provided flowers for the New Reichschancellery and even some fresh vegetables.

The New German REICHSCHANCELLERY

A very rare previously unpublished photograph of the finely detailed oak wood lockers Speer designed and had built into the quarters of the New Reichschancellery SS Guard Detachment. Note the ornate oak leaf shape of the hinges on the doors. The round black objects between the lockers on the left and the doorway are typical German bakelite light switches of the period. Below, a scan of an authentic piece of Rotgrau Schnöll marble from the Mosaic Hall in the New Reichschancellery shown at actual size.

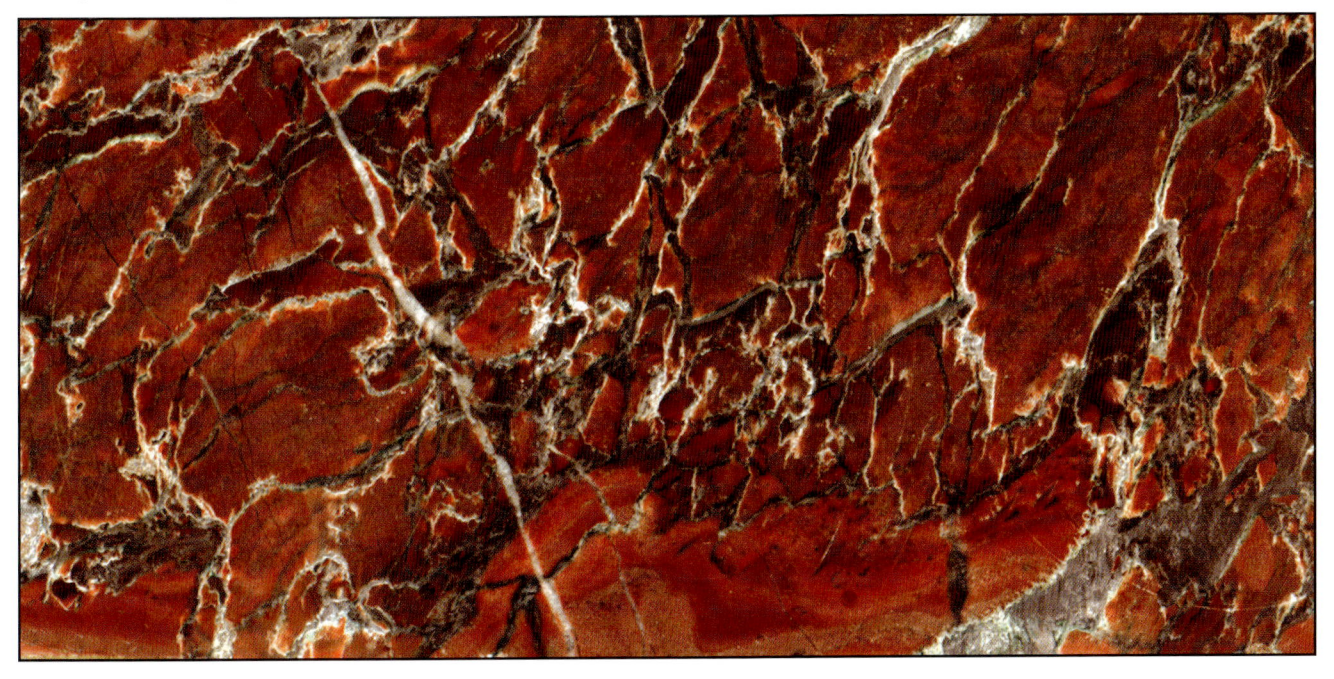

The New German REICHSCHANCELLERY

An excellent photograph of the front facades of the two Reichschancellery buildings built along Hermann-Göring-Straße to house members of the Leibstandarte SS Adolf Hitler Guard Detachment and some of the staff. Women like Christa Schröder and Traudl Junge, two of Hitler's secretaries, had small apartments in these buildings and mentioned them in their memoirs, which were published after World War II. In Christa Schröder's book "Er war mein Chef" there is even a photograph taken in her apartment.

The door between the two buildings is the entrance to the transportation and staff bunker beneath the New Reichschancellery garden. These buildings faced almost straight west with a view of the trees in the Tiergarten public park.

The New German REICHSCHANCELLERY

THE REICHSCHANCELLERY EXTERIOR DURING CONSTRUCTION

The picture above shows a special "tree" erected atop the center-front of the Voßstraße side of the New Reichschancellery in the "topping-out ceremony" on 2 August 1938. Notice that the crowd in attendance was standing amid large quantities of construction material in the middle of Voßstraße.

Below, a photograph of Adolf Hitler speaking to the 7000+ construction workers who built the New Reichschancellery. The thank-you speech was delivered during a special ceremony in the Deutschlandhalle at Messedamm 26 in Berlin.

The picture above was taken following a speech by architect C. Piepenburg. The crowd of construction workers at the "topping-out ceremony" (a traditional German event that signifies that the structure is completed and only finish work remains to be done), gave an enthusiastic salute and a "Sieg Heil!".

Below, a nice mid-morning photograph of the Voßstraße 4 entrance to the New Reichschancellery before the steps were ever finished. It is always possible to determine which of the two Voßstraße entrances to the New Reichschancellery (Number 4 or Number 6) one is looking at, as the enormous Schmid-Ehmen eagles above the columns faced each other. They are often misidentified in photographs.

The New German REICHSCHANCELLERY

CONSTRUCTION OF THE
in pencil drawings

1) The Voßstraße 4 entrance on the east end of the New Reichschancellery as seen from the top of a building across Voßstraße from the former Borsig Palace. Notice the glass roof already in place over the Mosaic Hall, and the Wertheim Department Store in the extreme upper left corner.

2) The Marble Gallery under construction above the air raid bunkers that were being built for the Reichschancellery staff.

3) The center section and east end of the New Reichschancellery with scaffolding along Voßstraße. You can see the same glass roof over the Mosaic Hall on the left that can be seen in

NEW REICHSCHANCELLERY
by Curt Winkler

the upper right portion of illustration 1.

4) Looking east on Voßstraße as the New Reichschancellery facades begin to take form.

5) An interesting illustration during the early phases of construction, looking straight east through the Marble Gallery and into the Mosaic Hall with the buildings along Wilhelmstraße in the background.

6) This illustration shows a very interesting view of the construction of the north side of the Honor Courtyard and the buildings in the Reichschancellery garden beyond it which connected the 1929/30 addition to the New Reichschancellery.

BUILDERS OF THE NEW REICHSCHANCELLERY

Like every other large-scale public building constructed in Germany during the Third Reich, the New Reichschancellery was built and furnished in the same way it would have been if it had been built in the United States. Private and public companies were awarded government contracts to clear the site, to excavate, erect, plaster, paint and furnish the entire building. The list of contractors who worked on the New Reichschancellery project was a "Who's Who" of international, German, and particularly Berlin-based companies. Many of the firms that contributed to the successful on-time completion of Speer's biggest building later advertised their part in the project with great pride. This section of display advertising will provide the reader with a good idea of the range of New Reichschancellery contractors.

Above left, the stone cutting firm of Bühl & Reuther of Berlin-Tempelhof provided Dolomite for the facade of the Honor Courtyard, granite for the paving in the Honor Courtyard, shell-limestone for the Hermann-Göring-Straße facade, and Jura marble for the ground floor hall on Voßstraße.

Below, the German Fine Cabinetry Workshops of Heinrich Arfmann in Bremen and Berlin manufactured and installed the interior in the Reichschancellery library. Another advertisement on page 85 is from the firm that provided the steel shelving built into the library bookcases.

The New German REICHSCHANCELLERY

NEUE REICHSKANZLEI · ARCHITEKT ALBERT SPEER · TÜRUMRAHMUNG IN DER MARMOR-GALERIE

Steinmetzgeschäft Köstner

Schönstraße 11   BERLIN-WEISSENSEE   Telefon: 562055

LIEFERTE: WERKSTEINARBEITEN IN KRENSHEIMER KALKSTEIN FÜR DIE FASSADEN · MARMORARBEITEN IN DEUTSCH-ROT IN DER MARMOR-GALERIE · MARMORARBEITEN IN JURA-RAHMWEISS IN DEN HALLEN IM ERSTEN OBERGESCHOSS

Köstner Stone Cutters of Berlin-Weisssensee made and installed the spectacular marble door frames in the Marble Gallery of the New Reichschancellery, and ran this beautiful advertisement in an effort to publicize their work.

The New German **REICHSCHANCELLERY**

PHILIPP HOLZMANN
AKTIENGESELLSCHAFT
FRANKFURT AM MAIN

FÜHRERBAU DER NEUEN REICHSKANZLEI

BERLIN / BITTERFELD / BRESLAU / DANZIG / DRESDEN / DÜSSELDORF
HALLE (SAALE) / HAMBURG / HANNOVER / KÖLN / KÖNIGSBERG (PR.)
LEIPZIG / MAGDEBURG / MANNHEIM / MÜNCHEN / NÜRNBERG / STETTIN
STUTTGART / BOGOTA / BUENOS AIRES / ISTANBUL / LIMA / LISSABON
MONTEVIDEO / RIO DE JANEIRO / SANTIAGO DE CHILE / TEHERAN

HOCHBAU
TIEFBAU
STRASSENBAU
STEINMETZBETRIEBE
ZIEGELEIEN

One of the largest, oldest and best known contractors to work on the New Reichschancellery was Philipp Holzmann AG. They rebuilt much of war damaged Germany, but by 1999 Holzmann was unable to pay its bills and needed a government "bail-out".

The New German RElCHSCHANCELLERY

MARMOR-
GALERIE

DER INNENAUSBAU DER STAATSRÄUME DER NEUEN REICHSKANZLEI

ERFOLGTE DURCH

VEREINIGTE WERKSTÄTTEN FÜR KUNST IM HANDWERK A.-G.

MÜNCHEN-BREMEN

United Workshops of München was an old consortium specializing in fine quality, artistic furnishings of all kinds. The designer/architect Paul Ludwig Troost had once been a member of the group. See photos on pages 38, 39 and 107.

The New German REICHSCHANCELLERY

WERKSTÄTTEN OTTO PLATO

BERLIN SW 29, KOTTBUSSER DAMM 79 • FERNRUF 622793 UND 629116

BAU · INNENAUSBAU · MÖBEL · WERKKUNST

Otto Plato Workshops made the table in the Hitler office photograph used in this advertisement.

The New German REICHSCHANCELLERY

Marcus Metal Manufacturing Company took pride in the enormous 3-1/2 x 7 meter (11-1/2 x 23 foot) bronze doors that they built and installed on the Wilhelmstraße entry to the New Reichschancellery through the Honor Courtyard.

The New German RElCHSCHANCELLERY

Kelheimer Parkettfabrik
Aktiengesellschaft
München
Werke: Kelheim (Bayern) / Berlin-Wittenau

✱

Ausführung der Tafelparkettfußböden in der neuen Reichskanzlei

---

50 JAHRE

SAALBURGER MARMORWERKE

Saalburg–Saale

Stahlkammeranlagen

Panzerschränke
Stahlschränke
Bücherei- und
Archiv-Anlagen

BODE-PANZER
Geldschrankfabriken A.G.
BERLIN – HANNOVER – HAMBURG

Above, Bode Armor provided fire proof safes for the Reichschancellery while DEUBA (below) dried out the masonry.

GÜNTER SCHULZ - BERLIN
LÜTZOW-UFER • 14

Maschinelle, seit vielen Jahren bewährte Austrocknung von Bauten in wenigen Tagen

Temperierung der Bauten während der kalten Jahreszeit mit erwärmter reiner Atmungsluft

„DEUBA"
Deutsche Bautentrocknungs-Gesellschaft m. b. H., Hannover-Hainholz

Temperierung und Trocknung des Baues der neuen Reichskanzlei

The New German REICHSCHANCELLERY

Elektrische Großküche
geliefert von der Firma
Gebrüder Roeder A. G.
Darmstadt

Vollelektrische Wäscherei
geliefert von
Ludwig Pfaff, Neu-Isenburg
durch
Max Lederer, Berlin W 30

Elektrizität

die lebenswichtige, allumfassende Energie findet

in der neuen Reichskanzlei

weitgehendste Verwendung. Außer ihrer selbstverständlichen Nutzung für Licht- und Kraftzwecke, für Rundfunk-, Signal- und Alarmanlagen, für Lufterneuerung, Kühlung, Eiserzeugung, für Personen- und Lastenaufzüge wird die Elektrizität als Wärmequelle vor allem im Wirtschaftsbetrieb in der elektrischen Großküche und in der vollelektrischen Wäscherei verwendet.

Auskunft • Fachberatung • Druckschriften

Berliner Kraft- und Licht (Bewag)-Aktiengesellschaft
Berlin NW 7, Schiffbauerdamm 22 • Fernruf: 42 00 11, Apparat 466 und 341

The New Reichschancellery kitchens and laundries were supplied and installed by different firms but the electricity came from just one company: Berlin Power and Light (BEWAG) Company.

The New German REICHSCHANCELLERY

Karl Groneberg

Feineisenbau

Metallbau

Kunstschmiede

BERLIN-LICHTENBERG

Eitelstr. 11-15 / Fernruf: Sammelnummer 55 05 33

Feinkonstruktionen

in Eisen, Bronze, Aluminium, aluminiumeloxiert und anderen Metallen

Treppen, Treppengeländer, Gitter, Tore, Türen und Eingänge

Beschläge

und Anschlägerarbeiten in allen Metallarten für sämtl. Türen sowie einen Bauteil Fenster

Sonderanfertigung: Verdeckt liegende Zapfenbänder mit Anschlag (D. R. G. M)

Bild unten: Tür in Bronze
Bild oben: Edelholztür mit Spezialbeschlag (Verdeckt liegende Bänder mit Anschlag)

Fine quality interior and exterior metal doors for the New Reichschancellery were made and installed by the company Karl Groneberg of Berlin-Lichtenberg.

The New German RЕICHSCHANCELLERY

Büromöbel aus Stahl

Schutz gegen Feuer und Diebstahl

60 jährige Erfahrung

Empfehlung: Lieferungen an Parteidienststellen, Reich, Länder und Behörden, alte und neue Reichskanzlei

Neue Reichskanzlei: Blödner-Bibliothek-Anlage aus Stahl (außer anderen Lieferungen)
Entwurf: Architekt F. Cäsar Pinnau, Berlin
Holzverkleidung: Holzkunstwerkstätten Bremen

AUGUST BLÖDNER / GOTHA

Spezialfabrik für Büromöbel

und Bibliothekeinrichtungen aus Stahl

Diroll'sche Natursteinwerke
MAX DIROLL
Burgkunstadt (Obfr.)

Kleinziegenfelder Kalkstein (Dolomit), grau, braun, gelb
Kleinziegenfelder Marmor, gelb, blau=grünlich

Bau der neuen Reichskanzlei, Berlin:
Lieferung der Fassade Ehrenhof und Innenarbeiten in Dolomit und Marmor

Münchener Gobelin=Manufaktur G.m.b.H.
MÜNCHEN - NYMPHENBURG

ANFERTIGUNG VON

WANDGOBELINS, MÖBELBEZÜGEN UND BODENTEPPICHEN NACH ANTIKEN VORLAGEN UND MODERNEN ENTWÜRFEN / REPARATUR BESCHÄDIGTER STÜCKE

„LEINS"-Spezial-Rolladenanlage

mit elektrischem Antrieb

– vielfach bewährt; auch für den Luftschutz –

ausgeführt u. a.

in den Empfangssälen der neuen Reichskanzlei

von **C. LEINS & CIE., STUTTGART** Gegr. 1886

Fabrik für Holz-, Wellblech- und Panzerrolladen

The firm of August Blödner of Gotha provided steel shelving components for the New Reichschancellery library. Parts of the Honor Courtyard were finished in Dolomite limestone supplied by Max Diroll from Oberfranken, and the Münchener Gobelin Manufacturing Company supplied tapestries.

The New German RERCHSCHANCELLERY

Gründungsjahr 1882

Carl Schilling / Hausteinwerke

Fernruf für Berlin 31 33 32 **Berlin-Charlottenburg 2, Schillerstraße 3**

Steinbrüche, Werkplätze, Sägereien sowie sonstige maschinelle Anlagen in

Kirchheim bei Würzburg – Muschelkalkstein

Wünschelburg in Schlesien (Heuscheuer) – Sandstein

Wiechs am Randen – Kalkstein

Steinmetz- u. Bildhauerarbeiten in Natursteinen

Lieferungen u. a. in den letzten Jahren:

Städt. Feuersozietät, Berlin

Erweiterungsbau der Reichsbahndirektion, Berlin

Verwaltungsgebäude
Preuß. Elektrizitäts A-G., Berlin

Reichshauptbank, Berlin

Verwaltungsgebäude O. B. R., Berlin

Beteiligt an Lieferungen u. a. für folgende Objekte:

Neue Reichskanzlei, Berlin

Reichsluftfahrtministerium, Berlin

Reichssportfeld, Berlin

NSDAP.-Bauten in Nürnberg, Weimar, Königsberg i. Pr.

Bauten für die Heeres- und Luftwaffe

Regierungsgebäude, Köslin

Regierungsgebäude, Breslau

Brücken zur Reichsautobahn

The quarries of Carl Schilling supplied stone for Albert Speer's New Reichschancellery. They specialized in shell limestone from Würzburg, sandstone from Wünschelburg and limestone from Wiechs am Randen.

The New German Reichschancellery

DRÄGER

Luftschutzraum-
Belüftungsanlage

in der

neuen Reichskanzlei

DRÄGERWERK

LÜBECK

BERLIN W 35 · ESSEN-RUHR · BEUTHEN 6-S
MÜNCHEN 13

Dräger supplied the air filtration and ventilation equipment for the bunkers below the New Reichschancellery while Zeiss supplied architectural glass used in at least six different rooms.

ZEISS SPIEGELLICHT

in der neuen

REICHSKANZLEI

ANSTRAHLUNG

MOSAIKSAAL

KUPPELSAAL

WANDELHALLE

WARTEZIMMER

MODELLSAAL

ZEISS IKON

ZEISS IKON AG

GOERZWERK · BERLIN

The New German REICHSCHANCELLERY

LICHTTRÄGER · REICHSKANZLEI · BERLIN

Kunsthandwerkliche Werkstätten Spinn
Berlin-SW68 · Alte Jakobstraße 133
Künstlerische Leitung: Kunsthandwerker Franz Haegele

Ausgeführte Objekte:
REICHSKANZLEI · PROPAGANDA-MINISTERIUM · LUFTFAHRTMINISTERIUM · INNENMINISTERIUM · KARINHALL · HAUS DER FLIEGER · DOM HEINRICHS DES LÖWEN
RUSTHOCHSCHULE / BRAUNSCHWEIG · RATHAUS BERLIN

The New German REICHSCHANCELLERY

NEUE REICHSKANZLEI
ARCHITEKT ALBERT SPEER

*Sitzungssaal
der Kanzlei des Führers
Deutsch Nußbaum matt
Bezüge blau Saffian mit
Goldprägung*

Entwurf: Architekt Cäsar F. Pinnau, Berlin

Ausführung:

**Bayr. Kunstmöbelfabrik
Willy Franke · München 25**

Many New Reichschancellery chandeliers, including the one on the facing page, were manufactured by the famous Spinn Workshops of Berlin. The Bavarian Custom Furniture Shops of Willy Franke in München furnished the Conference Room in the Chancellery of the Führer, as shown above. The furniture was made of German walnut with blue and gold upholstry. Otis supplied elevators not only for the New Reichschancellery, but for many Nazi Party and German government buildings as well, as you can see in their advertisement at the right. Below, is an advertisement for Pössenbacher upholstered chairs, made in München but popular in Berlin, on the Obersalzberg and elsewhere in Hitler's Third Reich Germany. The firm of Priessmann Bauer & Company of München supplied metal castings.

PÖSSENBACHER
MÜNCHEN   JAHNSTR. 45

Unsere Aufzüge

in der

neuen Reichskanzlei

und in den Spitzenbauten des Reiches:

Reichsleitung der NSDAP.
Reichszeugmeisterei / Reichsforstmeisterei
Reichsnährstand / Reichsjugendführung
Reichsluftfahrtministerium
Burggemeinde der Alten Garde der NSDAP.
Deutschlandhalle / Deutsches Haus, Paris
Emmi-Göring-Stift / Winnifried-Wagner-Heim
Haus des Fremdenverkehrs

sowie zahlreiche Lieferungen an Reichs-, Landes-, Heeres-, Marinen- und Flughafenbauämtern sind

**Spitzenleistungen
der Aufzugstechnik**

OTIS AUFZUGSWERKE G.M.B.H.
Zweigniederlassungen in allen bedeut. Städten

Priessmann Bauer u. Ci
Erzgiesserei
München · DACHAUERSTR. 76
TELEFON · 54539

The New German RElCHSCHANCELLERY

NEUE REICHSKANZLEI, ARCHITEKT ALBERT SPEER · MITTELBAU DER GARTENFRONT · SÄULEN AUS LAHNMARMOR »EDELFELS«:
HÖHE 10 METER, DURCHMESSER AN DER BASIS 1 METER

Marmor- und Natursteinwerke Josef Zander
DIEZ (LAHN) – FREIENDIEZ · BERLIN – WILMERSDORF
FERNRUF: DIEZ (LAHN) 243   BERLIN 861665

Marmorbrüche · Marmorsäge- und Bearbeitungswerke

The 10 meter (33 foot) fluted columns just outside the window wall of Adolf Hitler's office were made by the Josef Zander Marble & Stone Works in Diez. Facing page, the rare Austrian marble used for the interior of the Round Hall was supplied by Marble Industry Kiefer Company at Kiefersfelden.

The New German REICHSCHANCELLERY

NEUE REICHSKANZLEI, RUNDER SAAL IN UNSEREM OSTMARKISCHEN MARMOR AUSGEFÜHRT
ENTWURF: PROF. ALBERT SPEER, PLASTIK: PROF. ARNO BREKER

MARMOR-INDUSTRIE KIEFER A.-G.

BERLIN MÜNCHEN FRANKFURT a. M. KIEFERSFELDEN HALLEIN-OBERALM SALZBURG WIEN

KUNSTSCHMIEDEARBEITEN
FEINKONSTRUKTIONEN
BAUSCHLOSSERARBEITEN

aus allen formbaren Werkstoffen, insbesondere aus Leichtmetall, nach gegebenen oder eigenen Entwürfen liefert in solider Handwerkerarbeit und stilgerechter Ausführung

Der Kunstschlosser

KONRAD LINDHORST

Berlin-Oberschöneweide

Rummelsburger Chaussee 100-112. Tel. 634951, 631815

4000 qm Werkräume, vielseitig geschulte Gefolgschaft

Bronze-Haupteingangstür am Neubau der Reichskanzlei, Voßstraße

The New German REICHSCHANCELLERY

NEUE REICHSKANZLEI · DECKE EINER KANTINE IM SOCKELGESCHOSS

GOTTLIEB OLM
INHABER HERMANN LIPPERT
INNENAUSBAUWERKSTÄTTEN

RAUMGESTALTUNG UND MÖBEL NACH
EIGENEN UND GEGEBENEN ENTWÜRFEN

BERLIN SW 29 · GNEISENAUSTR. 45 · TELEFON 66 26 40

The firm of Gottlieb Olm made the ceiling in one of the staff canteens on an upper floor of the Reichschancellery, while bunker doors were provided by Mauser (not the gun company). Lindhorst made the bronze entry doors shown on page 92.

MAUSER

Frei!

Im Dienste des Luftschutzes

Der **Mauser** Notausstieg
für Schutzraum und Keller

Sicherer Ausstieg
auch bei stärkster Verschüttung

Schutz gegen Kampfstoffe

Luftschutzraum-Türen
einflügelig oder zweiflügelig,
mit und ohne Schwelle. Ausstattung mit den bewährten
„Certit"-Sicherheits-Verschlüssen.

Luftschutzraum-Fensterblenden

MAUSER K.-G. · KÖLN-EHRENFELD

**WERKSTÄTTEN
FÜR INNENAUSBAU** G.M.B.H.
WILLY HABERBECK
Berlin SW 29, Arndtstr. 34, Ruf: 66-9298 u. 9998

I. Internationale Handwerksausstellung in Berlin 1938
Medaille für hervorragende Leistungen

Bembé-Parkett im Reichskabinettsaal der neuen Reichskanzlei

Bembé-Parkettfabrik
Jucker & Co., K.=G.
BAD MERGENTHEIM

Mustergültige Werkstätten für feinste Tafelparketts

93

The New German REICHSCHANCELLERY

REICHSCHANCELLERY POSTAL MATERIAL

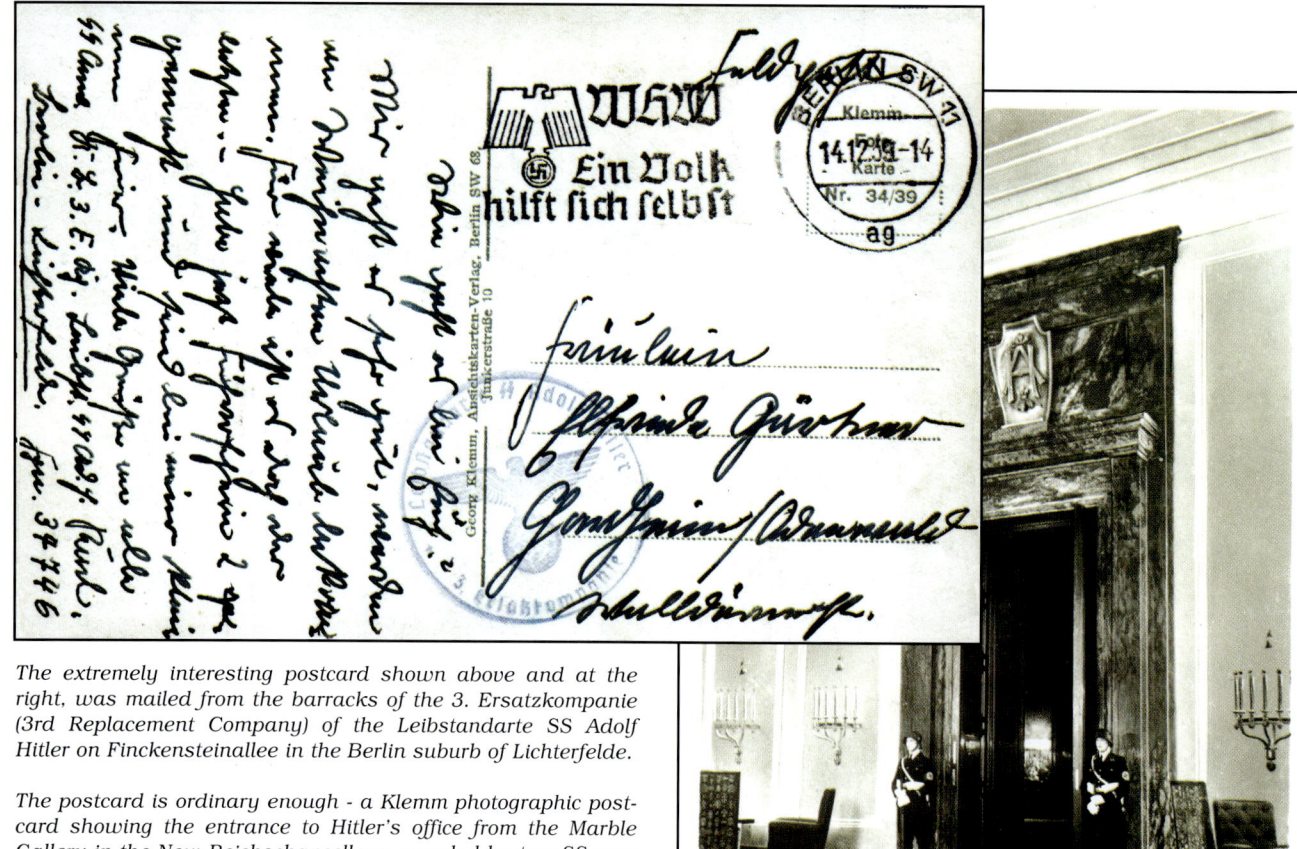

The extremely interesting postcard shown above and at the right, was mailed from the barracks of the 3. Ersatzkompanie (3rd Replacement Company) of the Leibstandarte SS Adolf Hitler on Finckensteinallee in the Berlin suburb of Lichterfelde.

The postcard is ordinary enough - a Klemm photographic postcard showing the entrance to Hitler's office from the Marble Gallery in the New Reichschancellery, guarded by two SS men of the Leibstandarte SS Adolf Hitler. The handwritten notation above the cancelation says "Feldpost" and indicates that no postage was necessary since the writer was in the military service. The round blue stamp at the lower center portion of the address side, is the Leibstandarte SS Adolf Hitler Feldpost cancelation and is shown in greater detail below.

The writer of this postcard was a member of Hitler's personal guard - the Leibstandarte SS Adolf Hitler, probably on duty at the New Reichschancellery. The postcard was mailed on 14 December 1939 to the man's lady friend in the Odenwald. It says: "How are you? I am very well! I will have a vacation at Christmas time. For many it will be the last one. I obtained my 2nd Class driving license and will have a small celebration. Many greetings from all of us. SS-Sergeant Ruhl, Leibstandarte SS Adolf Hitler, Berlin-Lichterfelde, Feldpost number 34746"

The envelope below was mailed from the Chancellery of the Führer of the Nazi Party on 19 November 1939 to the Reichs Ministry of Justice almost directly across Wilhelmstraße! No postage stamp was necessary because of the message in the little box under the round seal in the lower left corner. It says: "Free Handling Throughout The Reich".

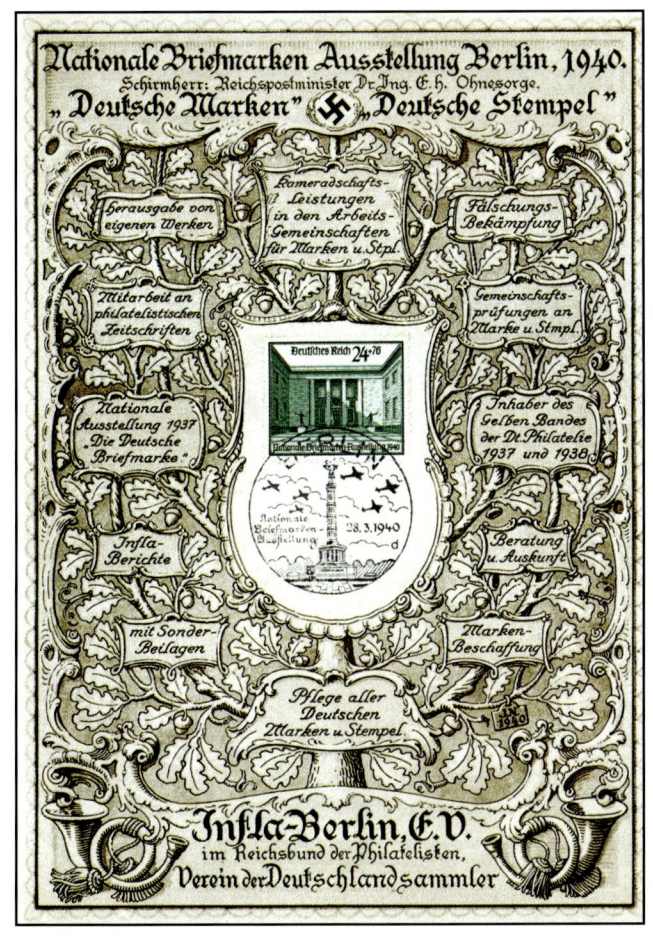

The New German REICHSCHANCELLERY

The beautiful engraved commemorative sheet shown above was produced and sold to stamp collectors at the National Postage Stamp Exhibition in Berlin in 1940. A close-up of the green 24 + 76 pfennig New Reichschancellery Honor Courtyard stamp and its cancelation is shown at the right.

The 9 x 12-1/2 inch envelope shown below was sent from the New Reichschancellery on 24 September 1942 to Mr. Johann Häntschel in the village of Schönlinde near Rumburg. It contained Hitler's certificate of congratulations on the occassion of the golden (50th) wedding anniversary of Mr. Häntschel and his wife. The words in the rectangle below the circular seal on the address label say that the envelope requires no postage for delivery to addresses in Germany.

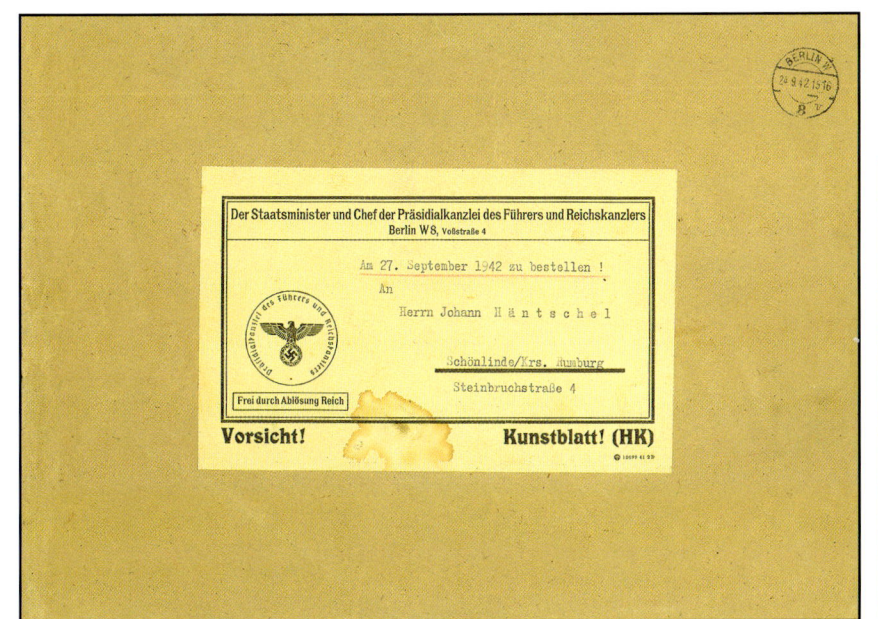

The seal below is a close-up of Hitler's official Reichschancellery seal as found on the back of the envelope. The certificate that came in the envelope is shown on page 96.

95

The New German REICHSCHANCELLERY

ZU DEM SELTENEN FEST DER
GOLDENEN HOCHZEIT
SENDE ICH IHNEN UND IHRER GATTIN
MEINE HERZLICHEN GLÜCKWÜNSCHE.
ICH HOFFE UND WÜNSCHE, DASS
IHNEN NOCH EIN RECHT LANGER
UND UNGETRÜBTER LEBENSABEND
IM KREISE IHRER FAMILIE
BESCHIEDEN SEIN MÖGE.

DER FÜHRER

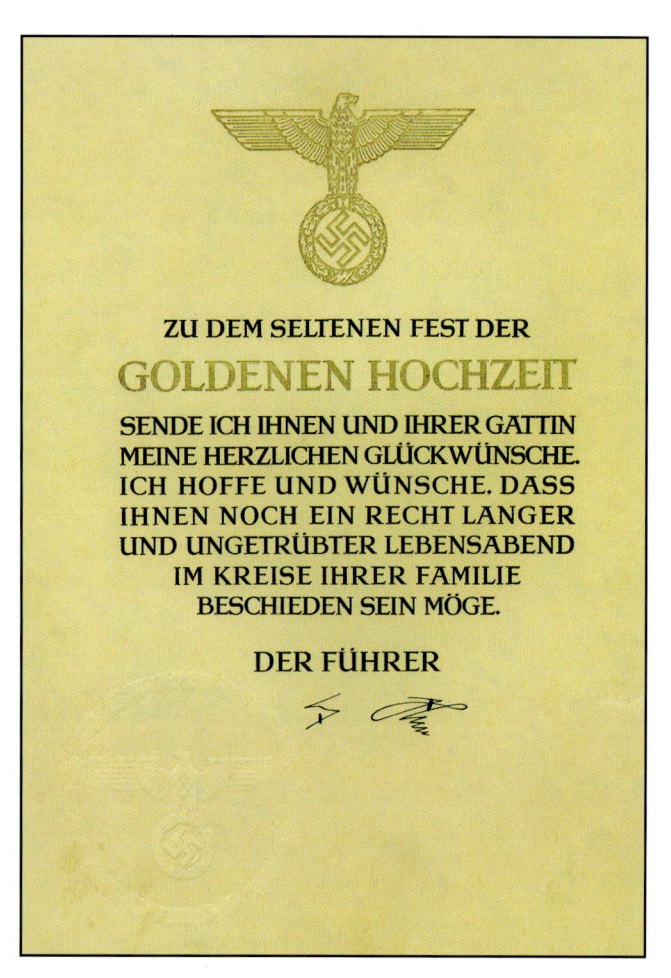

An official certificate bearing both the embossed seal and a facsimile signature of Germany's 23rd Chancellor, Adolf Hitler. This certificate came in the envelope shown at the bottom of page 95 sealed with the red and white embossed seal of "Der Führer und Reichskanzler". The certificate conveyed Hitler's heartfelt best wishes to Mr. Häntschel and his wife, as well as his hope that the couple would live a long and healthy life and spend the twilight of it surrounded by their family.

The five original Third Reich postcards at the right, are a sampling of a much wider range of Reichschancellery postcards that was available. The building was a popular subject, not only with government officials and employees, but with ordinary Germans as well. The photos are from top to bottom:

the Voßstraße front of the New Reichschancellery

the Honor Courtyard

the Marble Gallery

the Reichs Cabinet Hall

Hitler's Office.

LIFE MAGAZINE REPORTED ...

In a reasonably objective article in a fall 1939 issue of the American magazine LIFE, there was a feature on Hitler's *Berghof* mountain home at Obersalzberg, high above the small Bavarian town of Berchtesgaden. Over a picture of the house, LIFE magazine reported that, *"The rooms, designed and decorated with Hitler's active collaboration, are the comfortable kind of rooms a man likes, furnished in simple, semi-modern, sometimes dramatic style. The furnishings are in very good taste, fashioned of rich materials and fine woods by the best craftsmen in the Reich."*

The New German REICHSCHANCELLERY

The Leibstandarte SS Adolf Hitler received the salute of its namesake in front of the "Hof" or courtyard of the Old Reichschancellery on Wilhelmstraße, on 20 April 1939.

The New German REICHSCHANCELLERY

The New German REICHSCHANCELLERY

IMPORTANT DATES IN THE HISTORY OF THE NEW REICHSCHANCELLERY

Very dramatic events took place in and around the Reichschancellery. Among the most dramatic were the events of 19 and 20 April 1939 in celebration of the 50th birthday of Adolf Hitler, 23rd Chancellor of Germany. The photo on page 97 shows Hitler standing in his Großer Mercedes-Benz and saluting his personal bodyguard, the Leibstandarte SS Adolf Hitler under the command of SS-General Josef "Sepp" Dietrich. The photo was taken from the east side of Wilhelmstraße looking directly into the "Hof" or courtyard of the old Reichschancellery building. The photos on page 98 and page 101 were taken at the reception on the 19th of April in the Mosaic Hall of the New Reichschancellery when newly promoted SS Officer Candidates were presented to their Führer.

11 January 1938
Hitler instructed his architect, Albert Speer, that he wished to have a portion of Voßstraße cleared to allow the construction of a great new building that would be "especially impressive to 'smaller dignitaries'."

The funeral of SS-General and Acting Reichsprotektor of Bohemia and Moravia, Reinhard Heydrich was held in the Mosaic Hall of the New Reichschancellery. He was saluted for the last time by his two male children and Adolf Hitler.

2 August 1938
Topping-out celebration (see photo on page 73).

12 January 1939
The New Reichschancellery was opened to the Berlin diplomatic community with a gala New Year celebration.

15 March 1939
Hitler demanded and got permission to occupy all of Czechoslovakia from Czech President Emil Hácha.

19 April 1939
Adolf Hitler's huge 50th birthday party reception was held in the Mosiac Hall of the New Reichschancellery.

23 May 1939
Hitler explained to his General Staff that "Danzig was not [his] object", but that he would seek a total solution to the "Baltic problem" and the punishment of Poland.

31 August 1939
Hitler ordered German Forces to invade Poland in cooperation with the Soviet Union. The invasion was set to begin on 1 September 1939.

23 November 1939
For the benefit of his Army Generals, Hitler announced his unalterable determination to crush France and England and to ensure the neutrality of Belgium and the Netherlands by occupying them.

9 March 1940
Admiral Raeder, Feldmarschall Keitel and Hitler planned the occupation of Norway and Denmark.

21 May 1940
Admiral Raeder used Hitler's office to propose the invasion of England.

21 July 1940
A General Staff meeting ended with Hitler's declaration that he would "take the Russian problem in hand."

Hitler laid a wreath in front of the coffin of Armaments Minister Dr. Fritz Todt who had been killed in a plane crash.

14 November 1940
Hitler instructed Admiral Raeder to capture the Azores as an advance base for possible air attacks on the United States.

30 March 1941
To those assembled in the Marble Gallery Hitler said: "The communist has never been our comrade and will never be our comrade".

20 June 1941
Hitler ordered the invasion of the Soviet Union to begin on 22 June 1941.

February 1942
The funeral ceremony of Minister of Armaments Dr. Fritz Todt took place in the Mosaic Hall.

9 June 1942
The funeral ceremony of SS-General and assassinated Deputy Reichsprotektor of Bohemia and Moravia, Reinhard Heydrich, took place in the Mosaic Hall.

The photo above and the one at the right were taken at the funeral of Reinhard Heydrich in the Mosaic Hall of the New Reichschancellery on 9 June 1942. Above, Hitler salutes the flag draped coffin of the martyred SS-General. At the right, the German Chancellor adds the country's highest decoration to the many medals Heydrich already possessed. The photograph on page 101 is of the reception for Hitler's 50th birthday.

7 May 1943
The funeral ceremony of SA Chief Viktor Lütze took place in the Mosaic Hall.

20 November 1944
Hitler ordered his last attack - the Von Rundstedt (Ardennes) Offensive ("Battle of the Bulge") along the Belgian border.

16 January 1945
With the beginning of the Soviet Weichsel/Oder operation, the New Reichschancellery became the last German military headquarters.

19 March 1945
Hitler ordered the destruction of all German industry and infrastructure that could fall into Allied hands.

21 April 1945
Soviet artillery shells hit the New Reichschancellery long after it had been bombed by the American 8th Air Force.

29 April 1945
The 56 year old Chancellor Adolf Hitler married his 33 year old long-time companion Eva Anna Paula Braun early in the morning in the Führer Bunker under the Reichschancellery garden.

30 April 1945
Adolf and Eva Hitler commited suicide in the bunker under the Reichschancellery garden. According to Hitler's valet, Heinz Linge he disposed of their bodies in a shallow trench in the Reichschancellery garden by burning them and covering them with a thin layer of soil.

2 May 1945
Soviet infantry stormed the New Reichschancellery.

4 May 1945
The badly charred bodies of Adolf and Eva Hitler were discovered in a trench in the New Reichschancellery garden by Soviet soldiers.

December 1949
The last of the ruins of the New Reichschancellery were blown up and the remains were covered with soil. Stone and marble from the building were used by the Russians in the construction of the Soviet Memorial between the Victory Column and the Brandenburger Gate, their memorial at Treptower Park, and in the Mohrenstraße subway station under the former Wilhelm Platz.

The New German REICHSCHANCELLERY

The New German REICHSCHANCELLERY

REICHSMINISTER DR. LAMMERS EXPLAINS THE REICHSCHANCELLERY

As head of Hitler's Reichschancellery, Reichsminister and member of the Privy Counsel *(Geheimkabinett)*, Dr. Lammers was often asked to explain the work of his ministry of the German Government. He acknowledged that the function and position of the Reichschancellery in the Third Reich was fundamentally different from the Reichschancellery that preceded it.

He went on to explain ....

The fundamental changes in the Reichschancellery are a consequence of the *completely altered form and importance of the government of the Reich*. Before Adolf Hitler and the *Nationalsozialistische Deutsche Arbeiterpartei* [National Socialist German Worker's Party, NSDAP or Nazi Party] assumed power, the cabinet (which was an executive committee of the *Reichstag* or parliament) acted like a mini-parliament and the Reichschancellor was simply the chairman of that group. The cabinet ministers were directly responsible to the Reichstag so the Reichschancellor exercised relatively little influence on their various administrative branches.

Dr. Otto Meissner served in the German military administration in the Ukraine during World War I. In 1918 he entered the German Foreign Office and was Chief of the Reichschancellery during the Ebert administration. A confidant of German President von Hindenburg, Hitler retained him in the position of State Secretary of the Presidential Chancellery. Dr. Meissner's office is shown in the photograph on page 58.

Adolf Hitler on the other hand, in addition to his responsibilities as Head of State and Führer of the NSDAP, is also the supreme head of the entire administration of the country of Germany. He is therefore the supreme legislator. In former times, majority resolutions of the cabinet ministers acting as a mini-parliament, were the basis of legislative proposals and for the passing of bills by the Reichstag.

A majority resolution that would be contrary to the wishes of the Führer would be impossible in our Leader State. All laws passed in the Third Reich are formulated on the basis of complete agreement between the Führer and all Reichsministers. It is no longer possible for anyone to

Dr. Hans Heinrich Lammers, Chief of Hitler's Reichschancellery in Berlin. He was a veteran of World War I, a relatively early Nazi Party member, recipient of the Golden Party Badge and is shown in the uniform of an honorary SS General. Lammers was already a career government official when the Nazis came to power in 1933. When Lammers spoke, everybody listened!

introduce an unacceptable or inopportune legislative proposal, or to challenge a government or chancellor with whom they do not agree. Today, before a bill is submitted to the *Reichskabinett* for its decision, opposing views regarding its content and introduction must be worked out and it must be brought into harmony with the fundamental ideas of the Führer. The head and guide of the Third Reich is not an arbitrator, but a leader.

The headquarters in which all preliminary work on proposed legislation is carried out *is the Reichschancellery*. Obviously then, the Reichschancellery in the present Führer State is vastly more important than the Reichschancellery was in former times. To put it crudely, it formerly functioned very much like a correspondence office and little was done with regard to the settlement of differences of opinions or the content of proposed legislation. The Reichschancellery of today is the Führer's agency for information and the issue of orders in the administrative sphere.

Above all, as the head of the Reichschancellery I have to keep the Führer informed continually on a long list of important questions concerning legislation and administration. It is particularly important that the Führer not be sidetracked into dealing with minor matters and that significant problems be effectively organized within a chronological arrangement and according to subject so that they can be presented to the Führer in an efficient form for his examination and decision.

Regarding the representative duties of the Reichschancellery, the *Präsidialkanzlei* (Presidential Chancellery) and the Chancellery of the Führer of the National Socialist German Worker's Party, many people do not understand the difference. As previously explained, the **Reichschancellery** is the apparatus which gives the Führer information and issues orders concerned with the government's section of the administration of the state.

The **Presidential Chancellery** of the Führer has developed out of the office of the former *Reichspräsident*. It is headed by a Minister of State. In the Presidential Chancellery, those matters are dealt with which concern the Führer in his capacity as Head of State. Examples of those matters are official visits and receptions by the Führer for the heads of foreign states, the receipt of credentials and letters of recall from foreign ambassadors and the conferring of orders and other honors awarded by the Führer.

It is through the Presidential Chancellery that suggestions for appointments of officials are made, and pardons may be granted in criminal cases. Prior to these matters being dealt with by the Führer they have already been dealt with in their preliminary form by the appropriate Reichsminister.

The **Chancellery of the Führer** of the National Socialist German Workers Party is, as the name implies, the Führer's Chancellery as leader of the party. The Chancellery of the Führer is headed by a *Reichsleiter*, and it deals with all questions related to the Nazi Party, its sections and affiliated associations. It may make recommendations to the Führer regarding the acceptance of new party

NSDAP Reichsleiter Philip Bouhler was the long time head of Hitler's Private Chancellery until it was absorbed into the Nazi Party Chancellery of Martin Bormann in 1944.

members, complaints against party offices and officials, petitions for pardon in cases of judgment by the party courts, social provisions for party members and similar matters. Contained within this Chancellery is the Private Chancellery of Adolf Hitler, dealing with matters concerning the Führer as a private individual.

Quite naturally, the authority of the three Chancelleries of the Führer overlap in some cases. Difficulties that may arise in this way are rapidly worked out through the close cooperation and mutual confidence of the officials concerned.

Translation Copyright © 2003 by Ray & Josephine Cowdery

The New German REICHSCHANCELLERY

Voßstraße 6 before and after World War II.

EPILOGUE

General Eisenhower announced on 28 March 1945 that the war would soon end and that the Allies attacking from the west would go no farther than the Elbe River, and would allow the Soviet Army to take Berlin. That decision is often characterized as a "give-away". The western Allies held their Elbe front for nearly two weeks (less than 75 miles from Berlin) while the Russians lost over 20,000 soldiers in the capture of Berlin. What the Soviets got was a lot of casualties and lots and lots of rubble.

Albert Speer in his memoirs, mentions his last visit to the New Reichschancellery on 24 April 1945, and that "the effect of these [Soviet] shells seemed insignificant compared to the rubble that a few American daylight raids had made of my building during the past few weeks. I climbed over a hurdle of burned beams, walked under collapsing ceilings, and came to the sitting room in which, a few years ago, our evenings had dragged on ... and where Hitler's adjutant was now drinking brandy." The New Reichschancellery in Berlin had been reduced to a pile of rubble in just over

Soviet General Kotikov (right) ate all he could hold while many Berliners wandered the streets of their ruined city in search of food, housing and heat. Below, the ruins of the Reichstag seen through the ruins of the Brandenburger Gate.

The photo at the top of page 104 shows a couple of large open cars parked in front of the west entrance of the New Reichschancellery in the summer of 1939. The three-part front was the building's most distinctive feature. The lower photo shows the same building about six years later, as observed from the top of the ruins of the old Wertheim Department Store across Voßstraße.

The New German REICHSCHANCELLERY

Another remarkable previously unpublished Lieutenant Frank Knolle photograph taken in late summer or fall of 1946. It shows three German civilians under the famous "Speer balcony" on the 1929/30 addition to the Old Reichschancellery facing Wilhelm Platz to the east. The fact that huge pieces of the building have been carefully stashed along the sidewalk after rubble was cleared from the street indicates that someone may have intended to rebuild this building. Compare this photo with those on pages 13 and 18.

The photo below shows two of Knolle's buddies, Lieutenant Archie Patterson on the left and Lieutenant Charles "Bud" Avery on the right. They are standing in the entrance to the New Reichschancellery from the Honor Courtyard. The same columns can be seen in photos on pages 22, 23 and 25.

American Lieutenant Frank Knolle also took the superb previously unpublished photograph at the top of the facing page, showing his friends Avery and Patterson strolling through Hitler's Marble Gallery in the New Reichschancellery. Every square inch of the original Deutsch-Rot marble from the floor and the light colored marble from the window niches had already been stripped out when Knolle took this picture in the autumn of 1946. Amazingly, virtually of all of the original wall sconces were still there!

seventy-six months from its dedication.

The Soviets attached very little importance to the New Reichschancellery and very great importance to the burned out skeleton of the old Reichstag building. For this reason the bodies of Adolf and Eva Hitler were not even discovered until two days after the capitulation. Thousands of important documents from the New Reichschancellery and its bunkers were carried away as souvenirs or tinder before the Soviets discovered that this was indeed, the last German military headquarters.

At the conclusion of most of history's military conflicts the victors have found it in their own best interest to help the vanquished rebuild their damaged infrastructure. That was certainly not the case where the Soviet Union was concerned.

106

The New German REICHSCHANCELLERY

The photograph below shows a Soviet Officer explaining where Red Army troops found the charred remains of the bodies of Eva and Adolf Hitler, to British soldiers on his "tour" of the New Reichschancellery. For purposes of orientation, please note that the cameraman was facing south. The covered arched walkway outside the dining room can be seen in the background. See page 66.

The New German REICHSCHANCELLERY

The authors took this photograph in the mid-1980s from the West Berlin side of the Berlin Wall, at Potsdamer Platz looking to the northeast. It perfectly shows "the Wall" facing West Berlin (1), a second Wall facing East Berlin (2), and the no-man's land in between (3). Until we first published this photo in 1987, the mound marked with the X was *always* pointed out by tour guides as being, "over the Hitler Bunker". In reality, the Hitler Bunker was well to the east (right) beyond the black and white eastern wall.

Two previously unpublished photographs taken by the authors on 30 September 1986, showing earth moving machinery removing the remains from beneath the Old and New Reichschancellery in preparation for the erection of apartment buildings along Voßstraße west of Wilhelm Platz. The contents of the cellars was dug up and hauled away along with underground portions of the Reichschancellery itself. Voßstraße was south beyond the trees and sheds in the background of the photo on the left, running away from Wilhelm Platz to the right. The photo on the right shows Josephine Cowdery photographing the area of the Hitler Bunker.

The New German REICHSCHANCELLERY

Author Ray Cowdery in 1986 at the corner of Voßstraße and Wilhelmstraße in East Berlin, where the southeast corner of the Reichschancellery once stood. Beyond the cars were construction huts and beyond them, the Brandenburger Gate and the Reichstag building. See the photo above right.

Since the British government burned the US capital in 1814 there have been few more overt examples of the sort of wanton vandalism the Soviets visited on the capital of Germany. What could be moved and used was sent to the Soviet Union. The fate of German buildings like the Reichschancellery depended almost entirely on the use the Russians might have had for their components. Countless buildings damaged to a far greater extent than the Reichschancellery were rebuilt to their original specifications after the war. The Soviet destruction of the Reichschancellery was a capricious act of vandalism with few parallels in modern history. Today, all across Europe, buildings of far less historic value and buildings conceived and built with far less emphasis on quality by tyrants of all eras, bear blue and white protective shields designating them as *"UNESCO Cultural Heritage properties"*.

The New Reichschancellery stood in stripped ruins until the winter of 1949 when the Soviets blew it up. To fill a need for free construction material and to clear the site for other uses, the debris was carried away and the footings of the former New Reichschancellery were buried.

For many years the site of the New Reichschancellery was vacant from Voßstraße to very near the Brandenburger Gate along the old Wilhelmstraße. The clearing on the north side of Voßstraße was directly on top of the former Borsig Palace and Honor Courtyard and served as an un-

An unusual 1999 picture of the street sign on what is arguably Berlin's most historic street corner - Wilhelmstraße and Voßstraße. The unusual aspect of this photo is the presence of both signs! One or the other has been stolen repeatedly over the years. If you visit Berlin, please do not remove items of infrastructure like street signs. To do so is a crime, it is a great inconvenience to the public, and none of this sort of thing is original to the Third Reich period anyway.

Please notice the shape of the ß letters on these street signs compared to the shape of the same letters on the street sign in the photograph at the top of this page. The street signs in the top picture were put there by the communist East German authorities while the ones in this 1999 photograph were put up by the current city government of Berlin. None of the signs closely resemble the original signs of the Third Reich period.

109

The New German REICHSCHANCELLERY

This series of three photographs (above, below left and below right) was taken on 25 September 2001 by Andreas Gronemann of Berlin, as construction crews dug up parts of tile kitchen floors of the New Reichschancellery. The picture below shows the original white tiles on the concrete floor, barely visible between piles of construction steel. After sweeping away some of the earth that covered them, the remaining tiles were found to be in good condition. See page 83 for more tiles!

The upper right photo shows American Bob Wilson standing in the children's sandbox behind the Voßstraße/Wilhelmstraße apartment buildings shown on page 7. That sandbox is by actual measurement at virtually the precise spot in the Reichschancellery garden where Soviet soldiers unearthed the burned corpses of Eva and Adolf Hitler in May of 1945.

paved parking lot. Across the Wilhelmstraße intersection, the embassy of Czechoslovakia was built on the south half of Wilhelm Platz next to the Mohrenstraße subway station.

In September 1986 we visited the vacant Reichschancellery site in East Berlin for the last time. The sun shone brightly as workmen began excavating the extremely important and historic site so high-density dwellings could be erected along Wilhelmstraße and Voßstraße. We were shocked by the attitude that since the site was less than 50 years old it couldn't possibly be of any historic interest. It was as if we were watching an Egyptian Pyramid or the 1st century Amphitheater in Verona being torn down to build a shopping center. The difference to us is negligible.

110

The New German REICHSCHANCELLERY

So what did the Soviets do with all that building material from the New Reichschancellery? Well, they shipped some of it home to Russia, they built a monument on Charlottenburger Chaussee to honor the first Russian tank crews to enter Berlin, they built much of the monument to their war dead in Treptower Park (above left) and they allowed the East Germans to line the local subway station under Wilhelm Platz with marble cladding from the Mosaic Hall (above right). They renamed the station Otto-Grotewohl-Straße in honor of their communist hero. Today it is called Mohrenstraße station. After the erection of the Berlin Wall one could only travel east from this station. The tracks under the "Wall" to the west were blocked by the East German government.

As to the monument above in Treptower Park, Berlin tour guides invariably tell tourists that the red granite "flags" shown at the edges of the photograph above left, are made from material taken from the Reichschancellery. Not so! That material is red Swedish granite and it was purchased by the German government for use in a Nazi monument that was never built because of the war.

The eagle below was photographed by the authors at the United States Air Force Museum in Dayton, Ohio in 1986. It is the eagle mentioned on page 27 that was salvaged from the Mosaic Hall in the New Reichschancellery in Berlin by US Army Air Force Colonel Edmund W. Hill in 1945. It is a superb example of the genius of sculptor Kurt Schmid-Ehmen. Seeing it automatically brings to mind the question of why the government of Germany paid thousands of dollars to British architect Sir Norman Foster to design the eagle that looks like a turkey which now graces an entire wall of the new German Reichstag in Berlin.

NEW REICHSCHANCELLERY BIOGRAPHICAL INFORMATION

BREKER, Arno (1900 - 1991)

Born 19 July 1900 at Elberfeld (Wuppertal), Arno Breker became one of the most important and influential sculptors of the mid-20th century. His work on behalf of Hitler and the Nazi Party made it difficult for him to continue successfully after the end of World War II in 1945.

He attended the Elberfeld School of Fine Arts in 1918 and 1919 but had to leave in order to make a living. He became a commercially successful sculptor in 1922 and in 1923 visited Paris, France. In 1927 he moved to Paris and was quickly recognized for his genius by other artists, café society and the government. He successfully competed for valuable commissions and in 1933 won the Rome Prize which allowed him to spend a year in Italy.

Breker returned to Germany in 1934 and moved to Berlin. He won the silver medal in a competition for sculptures for the 1936 Olympic Games in Berlin, and in 1937 was appointed professor at the Fine Arts College in Berlin.

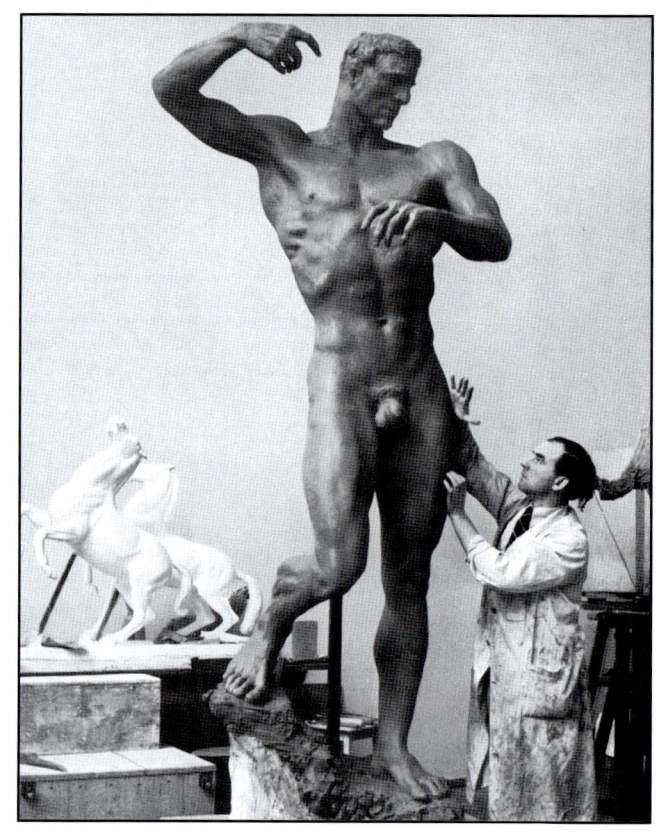

39 year old Arno Breker in his atelier working on a model for a sculpture of "Prometheus" for the garden of the Reichsministerium für Volksaufklärung und Propaganda (Ministry of Public Enlightenment and Indoctrination) in Berlin.

In 1938 Albert Speer chose Breker to create two marble reliefs for the Round Hall in the New Reichschancellery (see pages 30 and 31) being built at the time. Breker also won commissions to sculpt the statues "the Party" and "the Army" for the Honor Courtyard (see page 25) and "Thinker" and "Risk Taker" (see page 32).

In 1939 he received the Berlin Medal for Fine Arts and studied in southern Italy with Albert Speer, Josef Thorak and others. In 1940 he won the Grand Prize of Italy and became a member of the Prussian Academy of Arts and the *Reichskultursenat*. He also began working in a new studio at Jäckelsbruch and was visited by Charles Lindbergh.

With the capitulation of France only weeks after the German invasion in 1940, Hitler asked Breker to accompany him and Albert Speer on his famous early morning tour of Paris.

After the war, Breker and other artists were asked to publically express their regrets for producing art for the Nazi regime, which Breker steadfastly refused to do. In 1948 he was "de-Nazified" and

The incredibly talented Arno Breker in his Berlin-Grunewald studio at work on a bust of SS-General and head of the Leibstandarte SS Adolf Hitler, Josef "Sepp" Dietrich.

The New German REICHSCHANCELLERY

required to pay a token fine for being a "fellow traveler".

He worked in Düsseldorf and München during the 1950s, helping with the reconstruction and doing architectural work. He began sculpting again in Paris in 1960. In the 1970s, Breker received many international commissions and published his memoirs *"Im Strahlungsfeld der Ereignisse"*. He was very active in the last years of his life and died at the age of 91 in 1991. There are Breker Societies commemorating his life and work in Europe and the United States.

One of Kurt Schmid-Ehmen's fabulous Hoheitszeichen atop the German Pavillion at the 1937 World's Fair in central Paris.

SCHMID-EHMEN, Kurt (1901 - 1968)

Born in Torgau on the Elbe River on 23 October 1901, Kurt Schmid-Ehmen exhibited an obvious artistic bent even as a child. He attended the Academy for Graphic Art and the Book Trade in Leipzig and in 1922 studied sculpture at the Leipzig Academy as a pupil of Adolf Lehnert, while working as a stonecutter in Weimar.

Schmid-Ehmen moved to München in 1925 and enrolled in the München Academy working part-time in manufacturing and mining. Slowly, he gained a reputation for the beautiful busts he sculpted which were very widely praised. He exhibited publically from 1932 onward when he became a member of the NSDAP.

He received commissions from architect Paul Ludwig Troost and became one of his associates. Schmid-Ehmen created (from designs by Troost) the Feldherrnhalle monument in München, to commemorate the Nazi martyrs of the failed 9 November 1923 *Putsch*. Kurt Schmid-Ehmen's greatest fame however, came as a result of the many remarkable *Hoheitszeichen* (eagles clutching wreaths with swastikas in their claws) he created for Nazi buildings, arenas, grounds and memorials. They are among the greatest and most memorable monumental eagles of all time.

Schmid-Ehmen was member of the *Reichskultursenat*, the Reichs Chamber for the Fine Arts and the Prussian Academy of Arts. In 1944 he enlisted in the German Army as an ordinary *Landser* and was captured by the Americans in 1945. Few of his works survived the Second World War, except in photos. He died on 14 July 1968 at his home in Starnberg, Bayern, Germany.

SPEER, Albert (1905 - 1981)

The architect of preference during the Third Reich, who shared a love of neoclassical designs in a monumental style with his Führer, Adolf Hitler. Speer was the son of a very well-known Mannheim architect and studied the subject in Karlsruhe, München and Berlin. At Berlin University in 1930 he attended his first Hitler speech and he joined the Nazi Party in 1931 as member number 474 481. By 1932 he had received his first government commission and in 1933 he was given responsibility for the staging of the *Reichsparteitag* and other festivals.

Speer was an absolute natural at making the large look monumental, the grand look glorious and at getting masterful pageantry from an ordinary parade. In 1936 he asked for 130 huge search lights (the entire German inventory) to create a vertical curtain of beams (see page 37)

The New German REICHSCHANCELLERY

German Chancellor Adolf Hitler and his architect Albert Speer going over plans at Haus Wachenfeld (later the Berghof) on the Obersalzberg, high above Berchtesgaden.

around the *Reichsparteitaggelände* (State Party Day Grounds) in Nürnberg. He was surprised when his wish was granted and Hitler's only comment made plain that if Speer used 130 search lights for a visual effect, the rest of the world would assume that to be a small percentage of the actual German inventory. The lights could be seen in Frankfurt, over 100 miles away.

An extremely competent technocrat, Speer gained recognition throughout the Nazi Party and an ever increasing workload which he handled with ease. He was given the title Professor. By 1937 he was appointed the General Construction Inspector of Germany. In 1938 he became a Prussian State Councilor and was awarded the Golden Party Badge of Honor. He was a Section Leader of the *Deutsche Arbeitsfront* (DAF or German Labor Front) and chief of its Beauty of Labor Division. He was elected a *Reichstag* member in 1941 representing the district of Berlin-West. Speer was the head of the Nazi Party's Office of Technology, a member of the Central Planning Office and General Water and Energy Inspector of Germany.

The German Minister of Armaments and War Production, Dr. Fritz Todt, was killed in a plane crash in East Prussia on 8 February 1942 and Hitler picked Albert Speer to replace him. Replacing a trained and proven civil engineer with a sedate architect in the middle of the war would seem on the face of it to be a great mistake, but the job turned out to be tailor-made for Speer. He doubled and redoubled every kind of strategic production to the amazement of his friends and enemies alike. Analysts credit Speer's energy and ability with lengthening the war in Europe by up to two years.

In 1946 Speer was tried by the International Military Tribunal at Nürnberg and found guilty of war crimes against humanity. He was sentenced on 30 September to 20 years in prison and on demand of the Soviet Union (which had voted to hang him) served every day of the sentence in Berlin's Spandau Prison. Speer published his memoirs in 1970 and died in London, England on 1 September 1981.

THORAK, Joseph (1889 - 1952)

The son of an Austrian potter, Thorak was born in Salzburg on 7 February 1889 where he was greatly influenced by the city's baroque traditions. His freelance sculptures attracted prizes from the likes of the Prussian Academy of Arts and in 1928, attention from Adolf Hitler.

His muscular bronze and marble statues eventually adorned many Nazi building projects and in 1937 Thorak became professor at the Academy of Visual Arts in München. Hitler built a studio for him in Bayern where he completed models for huge sculptures for the German freeway system. Thorak continued his work after the war.

One of two sets of Josef Thorak bronzes of three figures each that decorated the stairway of Albert Speer's German Pavillion at the 1937 World's Fair in Paris. See page 115.

The New German REICHSCHANCELLERY

Professor Troost accomplished a great deal in the fields of architecture and interior design in his short life. None of his accomplishments were more significant than attracting the attention and the unbounded admiration of Germany's 23rd Chancellor Adolf Hitler. Hitler loved his simple, neo-classical approach to architecture, construction details and interior decorating.

TROOST, Paul Ludwig (1878 - 1934)

As a major proponent of simplified neo-classical building styles, Paul Ludwig Troost opposed both modernistic and regional styles. His work was greatly admired by Adolf Hitler long before the two ever met.

Troost was born in Elberfeld (Wuppertal) on 17 August 1878 and studied architecture and design in both Italy and Germany. He achieved significant fame around the turn of the century designing interiors for the homes of the wealthy and well-known. In 1910, he was appointed interior architect for the Norddeutscher Lloyd Steamship Company, designing the interiors for many vessels. In 1912 he joined München's famous *Vereinigte Werkstätte* and designed a wide variety of interior furnishings.

He met Adolf Hitler in 1930, and joined the Nazi Party immediately. From that point onward his time was consumed exclusively with design and architectural work provided by Hitler and the Nazi Party. Among his first commissions was converting the old Barlow Palace on Brienner Straße in München into the *Braunes Haus*, the headquarters of the NSDAP. He began to work at once on designs for the *Führerbau* (Hitler's München Office Building) and the *Verwaltungsbau* (Hitler's Administration Building), as well as the *Ehrentempel* (Honor Temples) built between them on the Königsplatz (see photo on page 23).

In the early 1930s he converted space in the Old Reichschancellery for Hitler but died on 21 January 1934 before he got under way with designs for the New Reichschancellery. The House of German Art in München was a Troost legacy opened years after his death. His wife Gerdy Troost, working with his assistant Leonhard Gall, completed work on many of his unfinished projects. Mrs. Troost, whose talents Hitler also admired, was given commissions to decorate Hitler's Berghof on the Obersalzberg and his residence on the Prinzregentenplatz in München.

THE PERSONAL STANDARD OF ADOLF HITLER

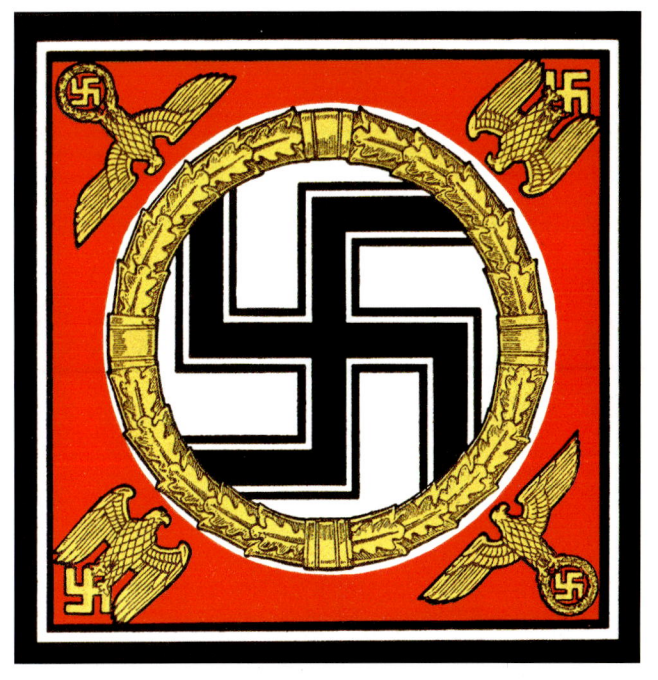

Adolf Hitler was both an experienced and competent artist before he served as a soldier in World War I. When he joined the Nazi Party, he designed its first flag and many of its insigne. He also designed his own personal standard or flag.

The colorful design above shows the "Führerstandarte" or "Standarte des Führers und Reichskanzlers". When Hitler was present in the Reichschancellery or elsewhere, the Führerstandarte was flown or displayed. It hung from the edge of his box at the opera and the symphony, and it flew from a staff on the fender of his car. Even the ribbons attached to floral wreaths that Hitler sent to funerals and other official ceremonies had a miniature of this Standard attached.

THE REICHSCHANCELLERY AT BERCHTESGADEN

Above, the Reichschancellery compound in the tiny hamlet of Bischofswiesen near Berchtesgaden in Bayern. This remote Reichschancellery was completed in 1937 and made it possible for the professionals from the Reichschancellery in Berlin to carry on their work during Hitler's extended stays at his Berghof on the Obersalzberg above Berchtesgaden.

The photograph below shows Hitler's Berghof on the Obersalzberg overlooking the valley in which Berchtesgaden lies. The town of Bischofswiesen and the remote Reichschancellery are located just northwest of Berchtesgaden. Below right, Hitler's office in the Bischofswiesen Reichschancellery.

From 1937 on there was a fully equipped branch of the Reichschancellery in Berlin in the group of buildings shown above in Bischofswiesen, Bayern. Bischofswiesen is just outside the small town of Berchtesgaden (pronounce *Bairk-tess-god-en*) not far from where Adolf Hitler had his mountain home, the "Berghof" (pronounced *Bairg-hOf*). It was Hitler's practice to retreat to his Berghof on the Obersalzberg for extended periods several times each year, and he took much of the Reichschancellery infrastructure with him.

The Bischofswiesen Reichschancellery was built specifically as a remote government center (sort of a "Western White House") and allowed Hitler to receive diplomats and to conduct government business without ever leaving one of the most

The New German REICHSCHANCELLERY

A photograph of a local couple awaiting their train beneath the Third Reich mural on the wall in the waiting room of the railway station in Berchtesgaden, Bayern.

beautiful places on earth.

Bischofswiesen, the Obersalzberg and Berchtesgaden are all closely nestled together in the sunny, rugged Alpine region of the state of Bayern, southeast of München. Geographically the area is one of towering mountain peaks, high warm meadows, sparkling creeks and a magnificent lake called the Königssee (King's Lake). We have spent a good deal of time over the years in the Berchtesgaden region in all seasons and it is stunning the year around.

Because of its relative remoteness and general inaccessibility, Berchtesgaden needed and got a new railway station in the mid-1930s. The new station facilitated increased traffic at a time when Hitler's Berghof was undergoing extensive remodeling and the remote Reichschancellery at Bischofswiesen was nearing completion. Visitors coming to see Hitler often flew or took a train to Salzburg where they could stay in one of the city's fine hotels. If the visitors were important enough they would be accommodated in the old castle remodeled specifically for guests of the government - Schloß Klessheim.

This recent photograph shows the huge Third Reich fresco that still decorates an exterior stucco wall of the Bundesbahn railway station in Berchtesgaden. The new high capacity station was built in the mid-1930s not only to accommodate Hitler's guests, but to facilitate the tens of thousands of Germans who poured into the area where their Führer had his mountain home. The fresco was denazified in 1945 by removing the swastika which had graced the center of the red banner held by the Bavarian defender with the shield. The sign below the fresco identifies the Berchtesgaden post office which occupies both ends of the railway station building.

117

The New German REICHSCHANCELLERY

A current photograph of the gates to the old Schloß (castle) Klessheim, just off the freeway on the west side of Salzburg. During the Third Reich the castle served as a Reception Center and State Hotel for diplomats and other high-ranking guests coming to see Hitler at Berchtesgaden, or to deal with the staff of the remote Reichschancellery at Bischofswiesen. Today, Schloß Klessheim is one of the casinos of the city of Salzburg, Austria. If you plan to visit, be advised a tie is required! Below are three photographs of the interior of the remote Reichschancellery at Bischofswiesen. Left, the Reception Room, top right, the Cabinet Meeting Room and lower right, the front entrance showing offices straight ahead and the strairway to the second floor.

Leaving Schloß Klessheim guests would travel by car or train on the short trip through spectacular mountain scenery to Berchtesgaden. From the railway station in Berchtesgaden it was only a few miles to either Hitler's Berghof on the Obersalzberg or the Reichschancellery at Bischofswiesen.

On the Obersalzberg, the Zum Turken Hotel was only about 200 yards from the Berghof, the huge Platterhof Hotel was on the road just above it, and between the Platterhof and the Berghof was a guesthouse for Hitler's private guests. Only the Zum Turken remains on the Oberslazberg today.

The Reichschancellery in Bischofswiesen was built from designs by architect Alois Degano. After World War II it was used as a US Army office building.

The New German REICHSCHANCELLERY

REICHSCHANCELLERY TEAPOT

The Sächsische Metallwarenfabrik August Wellner Söhne AG of Aue in Sachsen (in the Erzgebirge of east-central Germany) was a very major manufacturer of commercial tableware of all kinds, before and during the Third Reich. They had offices and showrooms in most of the major cities in Germany and in 29 cities around the world.

Wellner was famous for high quality, beautifully styled, extremely durable metal tableware ranging from gravy boats to platters, and tea pots to candelabra. They also manufactured champagne buckets, umbrella stands, picture frames, ashtrays and flag holders.

The illustration at the right is from the 1936 Wellner catalog and shows their style 6002, *Teekanne* or tea pot, above the logo of the company. This tea pot was available in Alpaca metal (an invention of Wellner - a silver metal that took and kept a beautiful polish) or in silver plated Alpaca metal at a list price of 53 Reichsmarks ($21.20) and 74.50 Reichsmarks ($29.80) respectively.

At the top of this page is a photograph of the same one-and-one-half liter tea pot with the emblem of the Reichschancellery on the front. It also has the capacity and the trademarks of the Wellner company on the bottom. Many people incorrectly assume that the tableware used at the Reichschancellery and other official German government food service facilities, was made of sterling silver. That is of course, preposterous.

There are many fake pieces of Reichschancellery tableware in collections and in circulation today. It is fairly easy to tell them from the genuine because the Reichschancellery logo on authentic pieces was "rolled on" at the factory with a steel die. Most of the fakes are made of 800 to 925 silver, were manufactured in Mexico, the Soviet Union or Cyprus, and have the Reichschancellery logo engraved on by hand.

THE LEIBSTANDARTE SS ADOLF HITLER

After being guarded by personnel from several elite paramilitary units, Adolf Hitler decided that the *SS-Stabswache* (SS Staff Guards) under Sepp Dietrich would assume the role of his principal bodyguards.

On 17 March 1933, the *SS-Stabswache* Berlin was installed in its new regimental headquarters in a 19th century Prussian Military Cadet School in Berlin-Lichterfelde. The men of the *SS-Stabswache* were given responsibility for much of the security at the Reichschancellery. Their leader, Sepp Dietrich, had his office and residence in the Reichschancellery in the center of Berlin.

At the *Reichsparteitag* in Nürnberg, held from 30 August through 3 September 1933, the 120 men of Hitler's *SS-Stabswache* and other special SS commands were consolidated and brought up to regimental strength of 1000 men. They were officially renamed the *Leibstandarte SS Adolf Hitler* (SS Body Guard Adolf Hitler or LSSAH). The LSSAH was never fully integrated into the SS as Reichsführer-SS Heinrich Himmler was never able to exercise command authority over Sepp Dietrich. Dietrich took his orders only from Hitler. On 9 November 1933, the entire LSSAH swore an oath of total personal obedience and loyalty to Hitler in front of the Feldherrnhalle martyr's monument in central München.

Enlisted members of the SS were required to be able to trace their aryan ancestry to the year 1800 and officers had to trace theirs to the year 1750. SS members had to be 1.78 meters tall (5 feet 9 inches), have an unblemished political past, and be good physical specimens with a Nordic appearance. As these requirements were far more stringent than for service in other branches, the SS certainly was an elite unit in that sense.

The LSSAH provided guard personnel for Hitler's aircraft on the ground, his convoys, along his parade routes, in his hotels, and of course, for the Reichschancellery. Typically, the Reichschancellery Guard Detachment consisted of a Commanding Officer, three Non-Commissioned Officers and 39 men. They guarded the entrances (including the entrance to the staff bunker/vehicle garage on Hermann-Göring-Straße), the garden grounds, the pedestrian subway under Voßstraße, the Honor Courtyard and the entrance to Hitler's office, but not to the total exclusion of guards from the *Wehrmacht* (Armed Forces) or the Reich Security Service. LSSAH Guard Detachment men traveled with Hitler wherever he went, especially to field headquarters such as *Wolfsschanze* and to the Obersalzberg.

LSSAH units took part in the campaign in Czechoslovakia in 1938 and the invasion of Poland in 1939 before the Waffen-SS (Combat SS) became a full-fledged part of the *Wehrmacht* in early 1940. After the German conquest of France, the LSSAH grew into a Brigade in August 1940 and into a Division in June 1941. LSSAH troops served with distinction throughout Europe in World War II.

An interesting pre-war portrait of SS-General and head of LSSAH, Josef "Sepp" Dietrich. Born in Hawangen, Bayern on 28 May 1892, Dietrich was a natural combatant and did not care for his early jobs working in hotels and as a butcher's assistant. He joined the army at 19 and served throughout World War I as a Paymaster Sergeant.

Like many patriotic young Bavarians, Dietrich joined the Oberland Freikorps and the Nazi Party after the war. His unquestionable loyalty, fierce nature and reckless courage was obvious to Hitler who placed him in charge of his personal bodyguard. A born leader, Dietrich was elected a Nazi member of the German Reichstag in 1930, given command of the LSSAH in 1933, and was appointed a Prussian State Counselor.

During World War II, Dietrich served as a Waffen-SS General and one of the ablest field commanders in any military force, Allied or Axis. He won the Knights Cross of the Iron Cross with Oak Leaves and Diamonds. His combat exploits in Poland, Russia, Greece, France and Hungary are legendary. Dietrich was imprisoned after the war for war crimes by the Allies, and later by the German Government. He died on 21 April 1966.

The New German REICHSCHANCELLERY

THE NEW REICHSCHANCELLERY TAPESTRIES OF WERNER PEINER

Hitler and his architect Albert Speer, were of the opinion that tapestry designer Werner Peiner was the rightful 20th century representative of the geniuses who created the tapestries of the Middle Ages. Tapestries were considered to be the pinnacle of monumental art. They brought a spectrum of color and shading, and a clarity of detail to grand scenes that would have been virtually impossible to achieve in any other medium. The picture above shows a Peiner design (one of six) for a tapestry in the Marble Gallery in the New Reichschancellery in Berlin. This tapestry was called "King Heinrich I Battles The Hungarians". The detail inset at the right shows some of the motifs Peiner was able to use in his Reichschancellery tapestries.

121

BIBLIOGRAPHY

Ambrose, Stephen, **Eisenhower and Berlin 1945: the Decision to Halt at the Elbe,** W.W. Norton & Company, New York, 1967.

Army Times Editors, **Berlin: the city that would not die,** Dodd, Mead & Company, New York, 1968.

Bach, Julian, **America's Germany,** Random House, New York, 1946.

Baedeker, Karl, **Germany,** Karl Baedeker, Leipzig, 1939.

Bennett, Lowell, **Berlin Bastion,** Fred Rudl, Frankfurt am Main, 1951.

Botting, Douglas, **From the Ruins of the Reich Germany 1945 - 1949,** Crown Publishers, New York, 1985.

Cowdery, Ray & Cowdery, Josephine, **Masters of Ceremony,** USM, Inc., Rapid City, SD, 1998.

Die Kunst im Deutschen Reich (magazine), Zentralverlag der NSDAP, Franz Eher Nachfolger, München, various issues.

Die Kunst im Dritten Reich (magazine), Zentralverlag der NSDAP, Franz Eher Nachfolger, München, various issues.

Die Neue Reichskanzlei, Zentralverlag der NSDAP, Franz Eher Nachfolger, München, 1939.

Die Neue Reichskanzlei, Kanter Verlag, Königsberg, 1939.

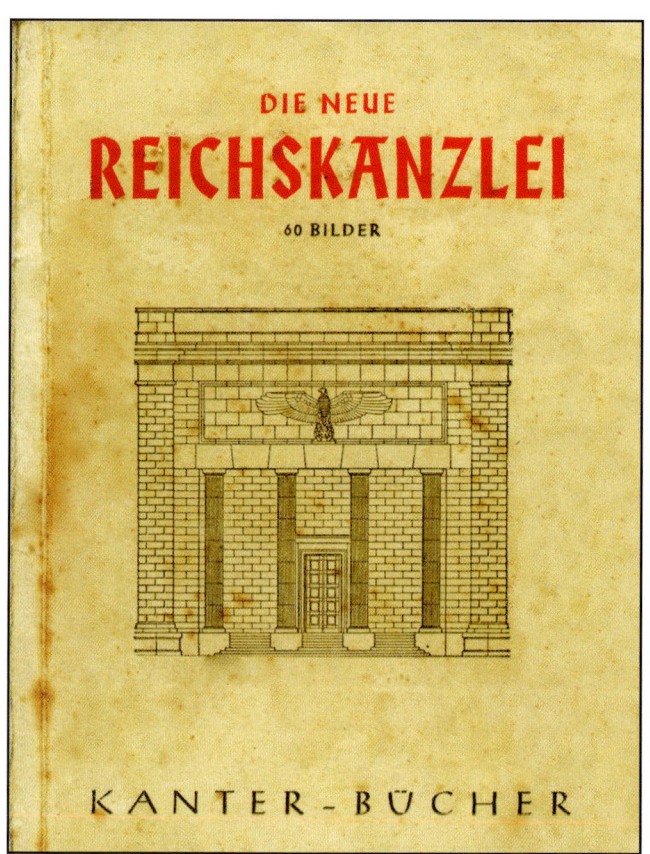

Left, the dust jacket of the magnificent 120 page, 12 x 15 inch, memorial book on Speer's New Reichschancellery. Above and below, a fine little souvenir guidebook that sold for only 90 pfennigs (36 cents), contained 60 photos and was popular with visitors to the Government Quarter of Berlin in the 1940s.

The New German Reichschancellery

Die Neue Reichskanzlei, special printing of issues 7 and 9 of "Die Kunst im Deutschen Reich" Ausgabe B "Die Baukunst", Zentralverlag der NSDAP, Franz Eher Nachfolger, München, 1939.

Freude und Arbeit (magazine), Verlag "Freude und Arbeit", Berlin-Wilmersdorf, various issues.

Gallante, Pierre and Silianoff, Eugene, **Voices from the Bunker,** G.P. Putnam's Sons, New York, 1989.

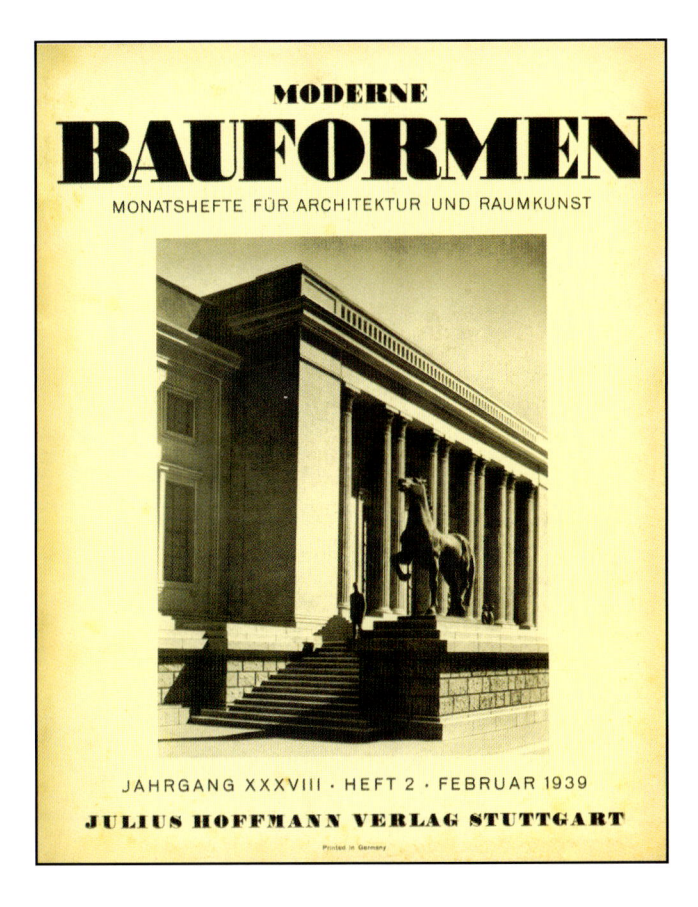

Three prominent German magazines which ran very comprehensive features on the New Reichschancellery that Albert Speer built for Adolf Hitler.

Hoffmann, Peter, **Hitler's Personal Security,** The MIT Press, Cambridge MA, 1979.

Moderne Bauformen (magazine), Verlag Julius Hoffmann, Stuttgart, various issues.

Orton, Peter & Scholz, Arno, **Outpost Berlin,** Orton Press, London, undated.

Schröder, Christa, **Er war mein Chef,** Nation Europa Verlag. Coburg, 1985.

Speer, Albert, **Inside the Third Reich,** the Macmillan Company, New York, 1970.

Theile, Karl H., **Beyond Monsters and Clowns - the Combat SS,** University Press of America, Lanham MD, 1997.

The New German REICHSCHANCELLERY

Last days of Hitler's bunkers

East Berlin workers with heavy equipment demolish what's left of Adolf Hitler's intricate concrete bunker system from World War II. The area, located in what used to be midtown Berlin, is close to the Berlin Wall and the Brandenburg Gate and will be the site of an East German housing project. Hitler committed suicide in the bunkers in 1945.

E. Berlin to Raze Hitler's Suicide Bunker

EAST BERLIN—The concrete bunker where Adolf Hitler shot himself as the Russians advanced into the Nazi capital is being demolished to make way for a park, East Berlin building officials said today.

"We are blowing everything up, every last bit will be detonated so no keepsake remains," East Berlin building chief Ehrhardt Gisske told Reuters in an interview.

Workmen are drilling holes for explosive charges in the 13-foot thick roof of the bunker near the Berlin Wall where Hitler took his life April 30, 1945.

The bunker roof will be removed and the cavity filled.

"We can do history no greater justice than by placing a park there in the middle of a wonderful housing area," building site chief Fritz Oske said.

We have intentionally omitted redundant information on most of the Reichschancellery bunkers from this book. The subject has been worked to death in countless books on the fall of Berlin. These two yellowed newspaper articles from 1988 tell the final chapter in the history of the "Hitler Bunker". The information quoted in them is of course, from East German officials.

IF YOU ARE THINKING OF GOING TO BERLIN ...

For reasons that are difficult for any well-read American to understand, the vast majority of Germans will go to great lengths to avoid discussing, or giving the appearance of being knowledgeable about, events that occurred during the Third Reich. Suffice it to say that laws in Europe make it difficult for anyone to speak his or her mind on subjects related to the Third Reich. Making any statement that may "incite racial hatred" is forbidden, as is the making of any statement that might "deny, minimize, or seek to justify crimes against humanity".

If you go to Germany, remember you are a guest in that country. Understand and respect their laws and don't engage their citizens in conversations that may prove to be problematic or even illegal. Do not take this book or other printed material dealing with the subject of the Third Reich to Europe.

The best advice we can give to those who may visit World War II related sites in Europe is this: study background material thoroughly before you go and mark your maps carefully. While you are there make your visits quietly and respectfully without attracting attention to yourself. Your interest in those places is not shared by more than a small percentage of Europeans.

Right, author Ray Cowdery searching for historical material in the "Fille Hof" second hand shop on Fasanenstraße in Berlin. This shop has yielded many Reichschancellery treasures over the years, but the owner has declined to sell the original Pariser Platz street sign that once hung near Albert Speer's office.

The New German REICHSCHANCELLERY

THE NEW REICHSCHANCELLERY AT THE RED ARMY MUSEUM IN MOSCOW

The Red Army Museum in Moscow, Russia, is the final repository for many of the items taken as war booty by the government of the Soviet Union from Hitler's New Reichschancellery in Berlin. The three photos on this page were taken by author Ray Cowdery in the Red Army Museum in 1976 and were the first photos of their kind ever to be published in the West.

It is a sobering experience for any objective historian to enter a room filled entirely by huge banks of the captured regimental standards of units descended from the most renowned *Traditions Regiments* in European history. It is awesome.

Between the banks of Standards lies the enormous bronze eagle by Kurt Schmid-Ehmen that was once the focal point of the Honor Courtyard of the New Reichschancellery. See page 22.

Unauthorized reproduction of these copyrighted photographs is strictly forbidden.

125

IMPORTANT!

The fold-out that follows includes plans, views, and sections of the most important portions of the New Reichschancellery. An examination of the drawings on the fold-out, the photograph of the model on page 10, the plans on pages 12 and 24, and the end paper maps should fully familiarize the reader with the layout of the New Reichschancellery.

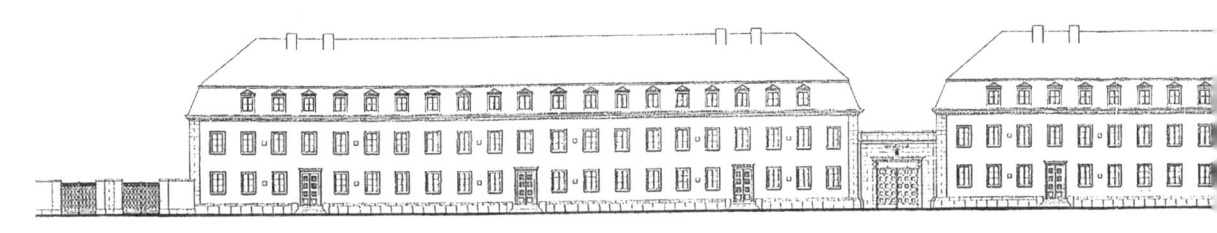

STAFF AND LEIBSTANDARTE SS ADOLF HITLER GUARD DETACH
(HERMANN-GÖRING-STRAßE)

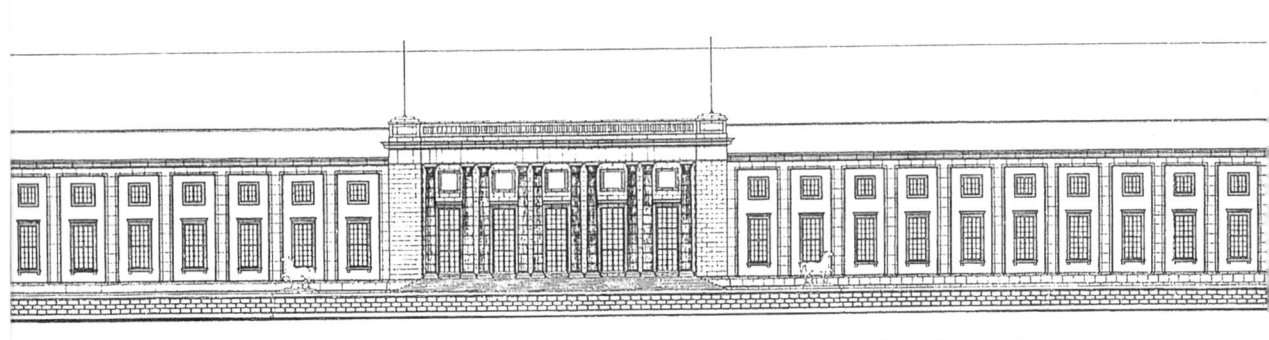

VIEW OF THE GARDEN SIDE OF THE NEW REICHSCHANCELLERY

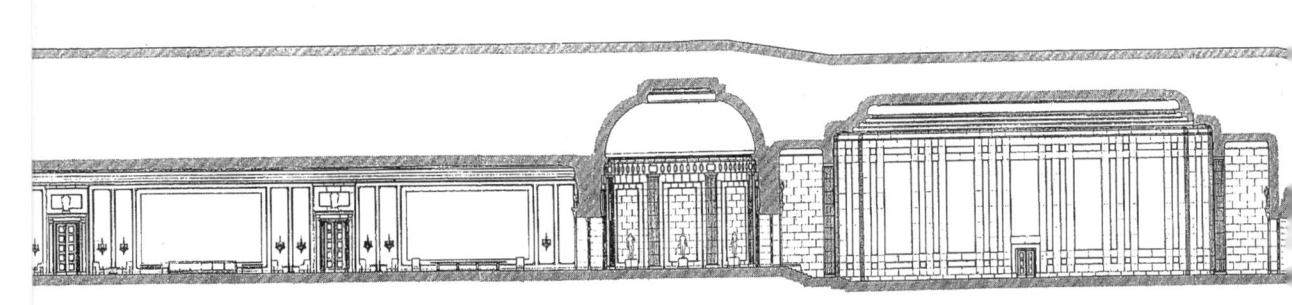

ROM HERMANN-GÖRING-STRAßE ON THE LEFT TO WILHELM PLATZ ON THE RIGHT

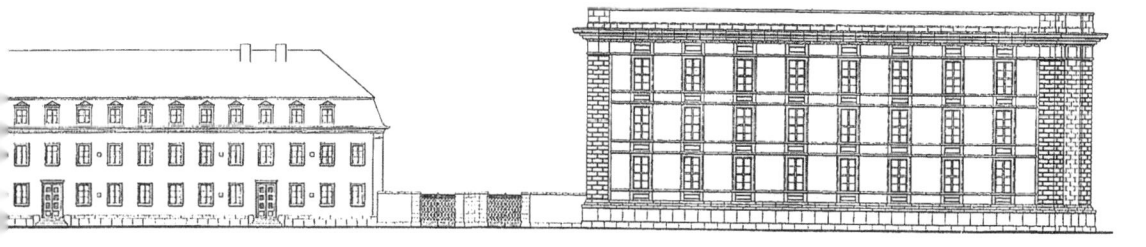

MENT HOUSING

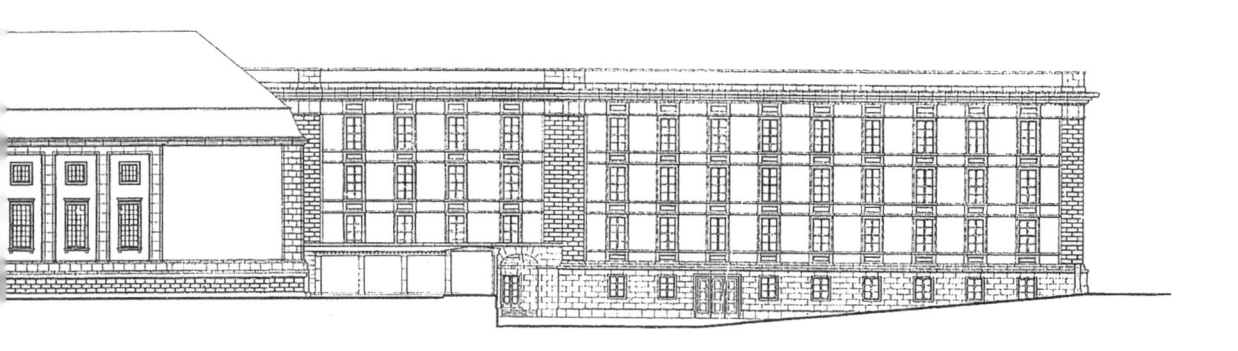

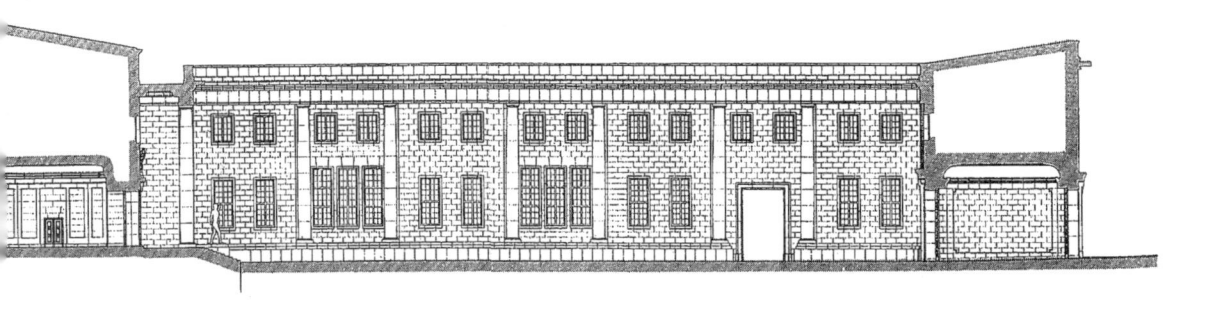

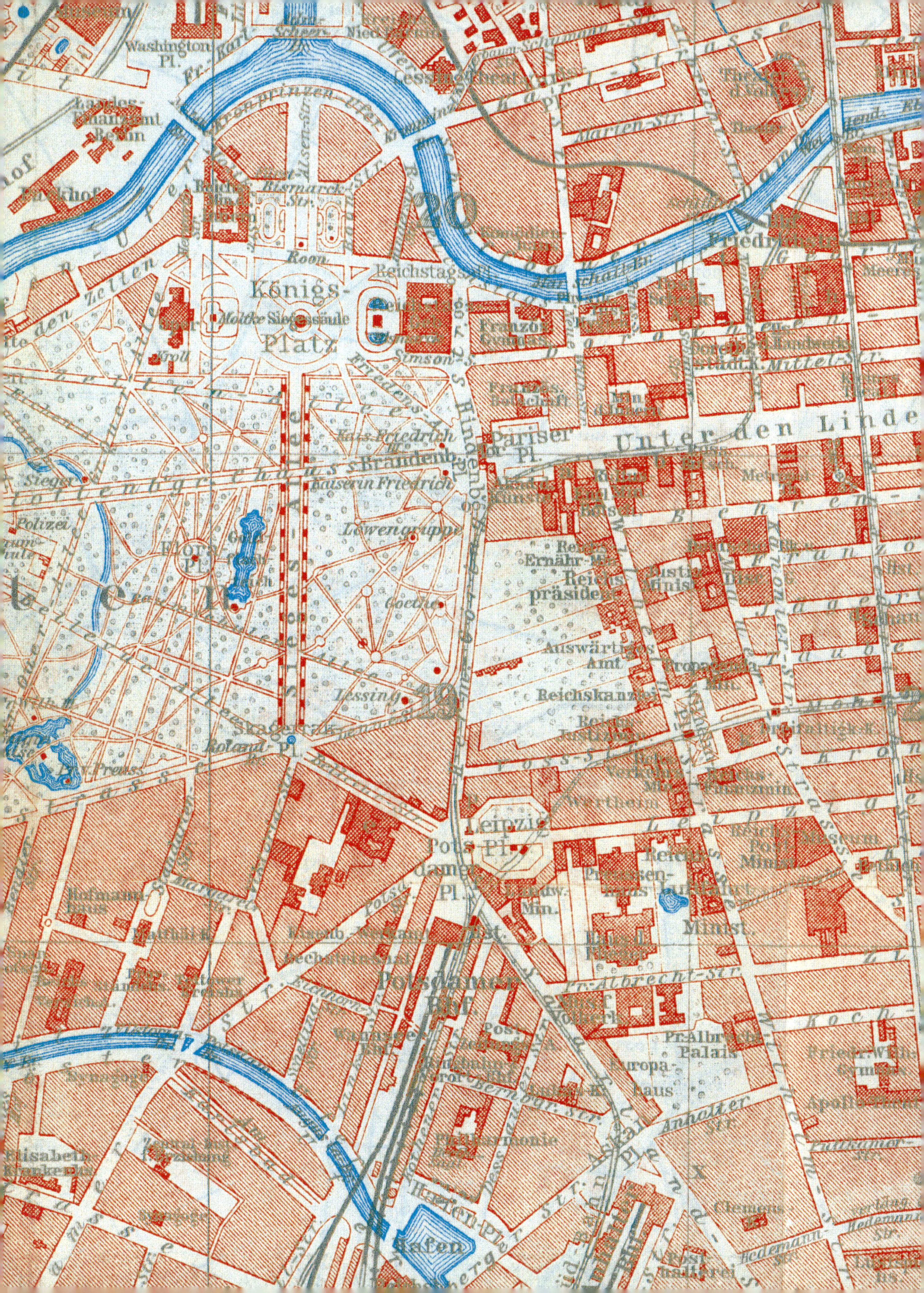

Washington Pl.
Kronprinzen-Ufer
Alsen-Str.
Bismarck-Str.
Roon
Königs-Platz
Moltke
Siegessäule
Reichstags
Simson
20
Pariser Pl.
Unter den Linden
Brandenb.
Kais. Friedrich
Kaiserin Friedrich
Löwengruppe
Goethe
Lessing
29
Flora Pl.
Polizei
Roland Pl.
Reichs präsident
Auswärtiges Amt
Reichskanzlei
Leipzig Pl.
Potsdamer Pl.
Wertheim
Pr. Albrecht-Str.
Pr. Albrecht Palais
Europa-haus
Anhalter Str.
Philharmonie
Hafen
Clemens
Koch
Hedemann Str.
Metropol
Behren
Ministerium